DIGITAL RHETORIC

DIGITAL HUMANITIES

The Digital Humanities series provides a forum for ground-breaking and benchmark work in digital humanities, lying at the intersections of computers and the disciplines of arts and humanities, library and information science, media and communications studies, and cultural studies.

Series Editors:
Julie Thompson Klein, Wayne State University
Tara McPherson, University of Southern California
Paul Conway, University of Michigan

———————————

Teaching History in the Digital Age
T. Mills Kelly

Hacking the Academy: New Approaches to Scholarship and Teaching from Digital Humanities
Daniel J. Cohen and Tom Scheinfeldt, Editors

Writing History in the Digital Age
Jack Dougherty and Kristen Nawrotzki, Editors

Pastplay: Teaching and Learning History with Technology
Kevin Kee, Editor

Interdisciplining Digital Humanities: Boundary Work in an Emerging Field
Julie Thompson Klein

Digital Rhetoric: Theory, Method, Practice
Douglas Eyman

———————————

DIGITALCULTUreBOOKS, an imprint of the University of Michigan Press, is dedicated to publishing work in new media studies and the emerging field of digital humanities.

Digital Rhetoric

THEORY, METHOD, PRACTICE

Douglas Eyman

University of Michigan Press

ANN ARBOR

Published in the United States of America by the
University of Michigan Press
Manufactured in the United States of America
⊚ Printed on acid-free paper

2018   2017   2016   2015   4   3   2   1

A CIP catalog record for this book is available from the British Library.

DOI: http://dx.doi.org/10.3998/dh.13030181.0001.001

Library of Congress Cataloging-in-Publication Data

Eyman, Douglas.
    Digital rhetoric : theory, method, practice / Douglas Eyman.
        pages   cm. — (Digital humanities)
    Includes bibliographical references and index.
    ISBN 978-0-472-07268-2 (hardback) — ISBN 978-0-472-05268-4 (paperback) — ISBN
978-0-472-12113-7 (e-book)
    1. Rhetoric—Data processing.   2. Rhetoric—Study and teaching.   3. Digital media.
4. Online authorship.   I. Title.

P301.5.D37E96   2015
808.00285—dc23

                                                                2014048158

Acknowledgments

This book would not have been possible without the great hearts and welcoming minds of the computers and writing community, many of whom show up within the text. I wish I could mention everyone who has had an influence on my thinking, my scholarship, my education, but the scope of a work like this is necessarily limited. I especially want to thank those innovators who started *Kairos* in 1995/96—Mick Doherty, Mike Salvo, Greg Siering, Elizabeth Pass, Corey Wick, Jason Teague, and Amy Hanson. I must also thank Michael Day for showing me the ropes at my very first academic conference and introducing me to many of the aforementioned innovators, thus setting me on the path that eventually lead to my becoming the editor and publisher of *Kairos*, which I believe to be one of the most innovative scholarly journals in any field.

And I could not have done this work if I did not also have excellent colleagues and editors who routinely make sure that *Kairos* continues to publish innovative digital rhetoric (as) scholarship and that each issue arrives in a timely manner. In particular, I want to single out Cheryl Ball as the true captain of that ship, but all of our editors and team members are critical to the success of the journal.

I am also particularly grateful to my colleagues and mentors at Michigan State University's program in rhetoric and writing, many of whom have read and commented on elements of this book in one form or another. There are too many to name you all, but special acknowledgment is due to Malea Powell, Jeff Grabill, Ellen Cushman, Bill Hart-Davidson, Julie Lindquist, Dànielle DeVoss, Dean Rehberger, and Jim Ridolfo. And, of course, my dissertation director, Jim Porter, who provided amazingly rapid and detailed feedback and made sure I finished my PhD in the four years for which I had funding.

Contents

Introduction

A common exercise in the first-year composition course is the literacy narrative—an autobiographical reflection upon the paths, interests, and practices that led the writer to the very moment of writing the narrative, focusing in particular on reading and writing as the pillars of literacy. A variation on this assignment, first introduced to me by Dickie Selfe (see Kitalong, Bridgeford, Moore, & Selfe, 2003), is the technology literacy narrative, which shifts focus from reading and writing to using and producing digital texts and the ways in which the writer has learned to use the technologies that support those digital literacies. I have chosen to begin this introduction with a version of my own technology literacy narrative, not because I believe that it is particularly unique or enlightening, but because it relates my intellectual development from writing teacher to digital rhetorician and in doing so serves the twin purposes of establishing my ethos as developer of this project and acknowledging that my approach to defining and locating "digital rhetoric" through the lenses of theory, method, and practice are necessarily both idiosyncratic and rooted in the disciplines through which I've traveled.[1]

Through my reading and research, I am aware that more than one academic discipline and intellectual tradition can make claims to being the "home" of digital rhetoric, and I've worked to make sure that I don't let my own history and bias situate it only in those traditions with which I am most familiar. In fact, I believe that digital rhetoric is an interdisciplinary endeavor that can as easily be situated in departments of communication or English studies and that can be performed within both broad, well-established fields, like media studies, and newer, more narrowly focused approaches such as critical code studies (the relationship between digital rhetoric and these and other disciplines and fields is taken up in chapter 1, "Defining and Locating Digital Rhetoric").

My technology literacy narrative wends its way from the early days of the personal computer, through a detour into using the mainframe systems in college, to writing my first web page and joining a community of scholars whose interests and work focused on the intersections of rhetoric, writing, and technology.[2] I will spend some time detailing my work as the editor of an online journal and the ways that my understanding of rhetoric (and digital rhetoric more specifically) were shaped by my doctoral program and the friends and mentors that inhabited it. Each of these elements serves as a building block in the long process that leads me to claim "digital rhetoric" as both location and scholarly identity. Following this history, I'll touch upon the problem of defining "digital rhetoric," address the question of audience for this work, and finally provide an overview of the goals and structure of the project.

Foreshadowing: Early Experiences with Computers

The first personal computer I encountered was the Apple II that appeared in my grade-school library (I was in sixth grade at the time, so it would have been 1979 or 1980). I was one of only a few students interested in using the machine, and I quickly discovered that one of the program disks was for a game called *Temple of Apshai*. In retrospect, I have noticed that the computer-as-gaming-platform has featured prominently in my continued interest in computers. I have always been more oriented to the humanities than to science and technology, but my interest in computer games helped me to see the computer not as a machine for computation so much as a new way to experience the stories embedded in the gameplay. Indeed, many of the early computer games I played were text-based adventure games, so I saw computers as reading-writing machines.

My interest in computers as tools for programming, though, really began in November of 1982, when I received a Timex/Sinclair TS1000 personal computer kit for my birthday. The idea of owning a computer that I could program (once I learned BASIC) was exciting not only because it seemed like I was participating in the world of the science fiction novels I read but also because I could bend the machine to my will through the use of simple programming commands.

But before I could exercise any power over the machine, I had to put it together. My first computer was also my first (and only) attempt to solder components onto a motherboard. My lack of success in this regard is likely the moment when I realized I was more inclined to learn about software and programming than to build hardware. At the same time, I believe it was a positive experience in the sense that I could see how the machine was made up of a variety of components; the final result may have been a literal black box, but I'd had the opportunity to see what it was made of. The soldering episode has also stayed with me because it reminds me that the digital is inseparable from its material infrastructure.[3]

A few years later, my family acquired a Commodore 64. Like the TS1000, we had to connect the computer's CPU to the family television, so my brothers and I would negotiate times to use it. On a very local level, the competition between user/producer (the computer) and receiver/watcher (the television) foreshadowed the perceptual split between interactive and mass media approaches to entertainment and connectivity during the 1990s and most of the first decade of the current century.

To the Mainframe and Back Again

In 1987, computers were not ubiquitous on campus. Very few students had computers at school; most of us had electric typewriters or basic word processors. At the small liberal arts school I attended, there were several computing labs around campus, each housing several terminals connected to a VAX mainframe.

One of my college roommates showed me how to customize my VAX account, send and receive e-mail, type and format papers for printing, and, perhaps most importantly, introduced me to the joys of staying up very late at night to chat with Japanese and Australian students using Internet Relay Chat (IRC). At the same time that I was exploring IRC, e-mail, and Usenet News in the campus computer labs, my creative writing teacher was experimenting with posting writing prompts to our VAX accounts: we were to read and write responses to these prompts (although the end product was still printed out, rather than simply e-mailed to the teacher).

These experiences taught me that using the computer and the systems it was connected to was a means of communication—the computer was not just a place to store and manipulate information or perform difficult mathematical and statistical functions; it was also a gateway that we could use to learn about and communicate with other human beings. It might seem natural to us now to see our computers as linking us with other people, as we use Facebook, Twitter, and webcams to communicate with one another, but at that time computers were not considered social machines (and computer *users* were often stereotyped as distinctly antisocial).

When combined with experience and the expectations derived from prior experience, the metaphor we apply to our computing environment is a powerful rhetorical figure that shapes our reality and potentially limits our understanding of how computing systems can be used: as late as 1994 I found myself trying to educate university system administrators about this facet of computing—that computers could be used for pedagogical purposes beyond word processing, programming, and computation and that the Internet had valid uses in a writing class.[4] In this case, the metaphor was of a single computing device rather than a networked communication portal. The lesson that I took from this experience is that how one is accustomed to using a technology tends to inscribe boundaries around acceptable or normal uses, and that suggesting new ways of using those familiar tools is often met with resistance. This same issue is also referenced in Hawisher et al.'s (1996) history of the field of computers and writing: "Before the computer could be seen as a writer's helper, computer users had to make what Bernhardt has called the *Copernican turn* (C&W, 1994) and come to see the computer not as a computational device or data processor, as it had been seen since its invention, but as a writing instrument" (46).

Before returning to school for my MA degree in 1992, I worked for a semester as a "community consultant" in the writing center at the University of North Carolina at Wilmington, which had a familiar and little-used VAX terminal—and I spent a good deal of time online when I wasn't working with student writers. It was through this connection that I discovered three things that would shape my scholarly interests and ultimately lead me to the field of computers and writing: an e-mail list of writing teachers who wanted to use technology in innovative but pedagogically sound ways (MegaByte University, or MBU-L); a text-based real-time interaction space similar to IRC called a MUD that hosted a weekly meeting of participants who posted on MBU-L; and a new way of storing, posting, and connecting information on the Internet using a program called Lynx to traverse the rather improbably named World Wide Web.

A Community of Technorhetoricians

Every Tuesday night, I would log on to MediaMoo[5] to join a vibrant and exciting group of people who were working in the field of computers and writing; these folks called themselves "technorhetoricians"—Eric Crump, founder of *RhetNet: A Cyberjournal for Rhetoric and Writing* (1995–1997), coined the term technorhetorician as a kind of shorthand for "rhetor-who-happens-to-study-the-rhetorical-features-of-technological-environments" (Crump, qtd. in Doherty, 2001).[6] I had created a character on MediaMoo and would go to the "Technorhetorician's Bar and Grill" to meet with the regulars—a group of quirky characters who were as interested in playing with/in these technologies as they were with seriously examining both affordances and limitations of these new applications for teaching writing.

In our weekly conversations, we discussed particular pedagogical approaches, asked each other technical questions, shared success and horror stories, and provided a much needed support system for people who were working against departmental and institutional resistance to their work with technology. Through my participation in these communities, I was introduced to the field's singular journal, *Computers and Composition* (still one of the best resources for work in computers and writing and digital rhetoric as scholarly practice), as well as a number of influential edited collections. Three of the collections that most influenced my own work (and eventually contributed to my understanding of "digital rhetoric") were Myron Tuman's (1992) *Literacy Online*, Hawisher and LeBlanc's (1992) *Reimagining Computers and Composition: Teaching and Research in a Virtual Age*, and Hawisher and Selfe's (1991) *Evolving Perspectives on Computers and Composition Studies*.

Tuman's collection features essays from a 1989 conference that focused on the impact of technology on literary studies; in each section two or more chapters consider the ways that computers have facilitated "new forms"— new forms of texts, new forms of teaching English, new forms of critical thought, new forms of administrative control, new forms of knowledge. It is in this final category that Richard Lanham's essay, "Digital Rhetoric: Theory, Practice, and Property," appears (the first use of the term and an important early articulation of making the connection between digital texts and rhetorical theory—an overview of this work appears in the next chapter). It is fitting, I think, that Tuman placed Lanham's essay not in the sections on "new forms of text" or "new forms of critical thought" but in the broader approach to "new forms of knowledge."

As with Lanham's essay in *Literacy Online*, I found that each of the other two collections featured a chapter that stands out both in terms of its influence on my scholarly interests and in terms of contributing to a definition of digital rhetoric. In *Reimagining*, I was first drawn to Paul Taylor's "Social Epistemic Rhetoric and Chaotic Discourse" through his use of rhetorics of science and, in particular, the application of chaos theory as a lens for considering the possibilities of transactional rhetoric.[7] Taylor's essay resonated for me in part because I was at the time also learning about theories of composition and reading Mikhail Bakhtin and Julia Kristeva, and he neatly synthesized all of these theories in the context of a case study of electronic conferencing in a writing class.

John McDaid's "Toward an Ecology of Hypermedia" in *Evolving Perspectives* leans heavily on Marshall McLuhan's *Understanding Media*, arguing that "media are not passive conduits of information, but active shapers and massagers of messages. To fully apprehend the character of the world they bring us, we must see them as an ecosystem: interacting, shaping, and re-presenting our experience" (204). McDaid contrasts rhetorical characteristics of orality, (print) literacy, and hypermedia (the literacy of which he calls "digitality") in terms of author, text, and audience and similarly contrasts the characteristics of oral, literate, and digital cultures via a matrix that includes media, mind, universe, culture, and technology (208–16).

These works were my introduction to the field of computers and writing, and between a rapid immersion in the scholarship of the field and my continued participation in the online discussions and e-mail list, I quickly became convinced that this was my academic home. My next step was to attend my first Computers and Writing conference, held in Logan, Utah, in 1996.[8] At this conference, I learned about the history of computers and writing (this was the twelfth Computers and Writing Conference[9]; 1996 also saw the publication of Hawisher, LeBlanc, Moran, and Selfe's *Computers and the Teaching of Writing in American Higher Education, 1979–1994: A History*). Perhaps the most important aspect of this conference was the time I spent with the founding editors of *Kairos: A Journal for Teachers of Writing in Webbed Environments*, which ultimately lead to an invitation to join the editorial staff.

The Kairos of *Kairos*

I joined the staff of *Kairos* as CoverWeb editor in 1997. The CoverWeb was supposed to be a multiauthored, multivocal cross-linked collection of individual webtexts that would focus on a particular theme in each issue (such as disability studies online or copyright and intellectual property issues). The CoverWeb was an interesting idea in theory, but in practice it never really lived up to its potential. In 2000 I became chief editor for a brief time and then served as coeditor with James Inman before finally transitioning to senior editor and publisher in 2006. In my current role, I am responsible for personnel decisions, big picture issues focusing on our mission and goals, and working to maintain the technical infrastructure. I make final corrections to all the webtexts and perform a code-edit before building each issue's table of contents and releasing the issue for public distribution. I am eternally grateful to have the indefatigable Cheryl Ball as chief editor—she works with the editorial staff, the editorial board, and the peer-review process, and she makes sure each issue gets out on time.

Kairos began as an experiment in scholarly publishing developed by a group of energetic and forward-thinking graduate students who wanted to see the web used to create new scholarly forms (there was some frustration with reading the work of scholars who were adept at critiquing these new kinds of online texts but who could not themselves produce anything like them).[10]

My own first article appeared in issue 1.2 and by current design standards, the best that I can say is that it is at least readable. But as the use of the web became ubiquitous, and more scholars began paying attention to and seeing value in learning about design and even coding, the quality of the work we published continually improved. We also shifted focus slightly, changing our subtitle from "A Journal for Teachers of Writing in Webbed Environments" to "A Journal of Rhetoric, Technology, and Pedagogy." We currently publish between two and three issues per year, and the acceptance rate for our peer-reviewed webtexts averages around 10 percent. As we have continued to publish innovative scholarly works, we have enjoyed increased popularity—we're currently recording around fifty thousand individual readers per month, arriving from more than 180 different countries.[11]

One of the more interesting aspects of my experience as editor of the journal is being exposed to such a wide range of design approaches and choices (even if those choices sometimes conflict with our technology standards). There are times when an author creates a work where the design really carries the argument, just as much as (or more so) than the text (one of the best examples of meaning enacted through design is Anne Wysocki's [2002] "A Bookling Monument," which required the user to interact with both text and image in order to really understand and "see" the argument unfold). There has also been a marked increase in the use of multimedia; we still receive works that are primarily print and code (HTML and CSS), but we are just as likely to receive work that is primarily audio, or video, or a combination of text, audio, and video. We have also published works that use wiki and blog platforms as well.

I will return to works that we have published in the journal when I address digital rhetoric practice (in terms of scholarship), as we have published a significant number of webtexts that both address and enact digital rhetoric. I would say that it is because of my work at *Kairos* that I first became interested in multimodal/multimedia composition and it was through the journal that I was first introduced to the many facets of rhetorical theory and method as applied to (and facilitating the production of) digital texts.

From Composition to Rhetoric to Digital Rhetoric

In 2003, I enrolled in Michigan State University's then-new doctoral program in writing and rhetoric. It was through that program that I began to fully apprehend the power and facility of rhetoric, and I shifted my disciplinary identity from composition teacher to rhetorician. One of the courses I took as a graduate student was called "Digital Rhetoric," taught by Dànielle DeVoss. Because there were very few works explicitly addressing digital rhetoric in 2004, the class worked together to develop a definition and shared understanding. As a result of that investigation, a number of students and faculty decided to create a digital rhetoric research collective that we christened digirhet.net (making a play on a URL while also calling attention to the notion that we could work as and in a network formation). The name has been fluid, like the networks we study, changing to digirhet.org in our first publication and simply digirhet in the second. Based on work in that course, our collective published an article on teaching digital rhetoric in *Pedagogy* (see chapter 4, "Digital Rhetoric: Practice," for an overview). Based on my experience at *Kairos*, it seemed a natural progression to decide that digital rhetoric is what I would study and what I would do. And so I did, and I completed my dissertation in 2007, which theorized digital rhetoric in terms of circulation in and through digital ecologies and participating in digital economies, revised portions of which appear in chapter 2 ("Digital Rhetoric: Theory") and chapter 3 ("Digital Rhetoric: Method").

Digital Rhetoric: Theory, Method, Practice

In *Virtualpolitik* (2009), Elizabeth Losh traces the term "digital rhetoric" to Richard Lanham's "Digital Rhetoric and the Digital Arts" (1992), which was an early influence on my own thinking about how one would define digital rhetoric. The next time I encountered the term was in an article in *College Composition and Communication* by Mary Hocks—her definition asserts that "digital rhetoric describes a system of ongoing dialogue and negotiations among writers, audiences, and institutional contexts, but it focuses on the multiple modalities available for making meaning using new communication and information technologies" (2003, 632). From my perspective, there had been a fairly extensive gap between Lanham's coining of the term and the next attempt to define and use it. But midway through my doctoral program, I encountered James Zappen's article on digital rhetoric, which serves in a roundabout way as a model for this text. In 2005, Zappen argued that current work toward developing digital rhetoric has thus far resulted in "an amalgam of more-or-less discrete components rather than a complete and integrated theory in its own right. These discrete components nonetheless provide at least a partial outline for such a theory, which has potential to contribute to the larger body of rhetorical theory and criticism" (323); this lack of "an integrated theory" seemed to me a perfect opening for my own work toward understanding, defining, and shaping a vision of digital rhetoric (although I have moved from seeking an integrated theory to articulating digital rhetoric theories and methods).

Although scholars such as Elizabeth Losh (2009) and Ian Bogost (2007) have addressed and critiqued the idea of digital rhetoric, no comprehensive digital rhetoric text has yet been published; thus this volume aims to provide an overview and synthesis of the work that has been done on the development of a digital rhetoric theory and also to provide a framework that situates digital rhetoric as an interdisciplinary field of inquiry in its own right. Depending on where the field boundaries are drawn, and what counts as digital rhetoric theory, it is possible to claim a fairly extensive literature as falling within the purview of the field: the term "digital rhetoric" itself has been applied to rhetorics of technology, network rhetorics, social media use, the use of rhetorical appeals in online discussion forums, website design, multimodal composition, and the study of new media (itself a contested term). If we see digital rhetoric as a productive art, then nearly all digital texts can be seen both as objects of study for analysis (using digital rhetoric methods) and as products of digital rhetoric practices. Rather than attempt to provide a comprehensive representation of all that is or could be digital rhetoric, I have chosen to be fairly selective in my overview, first considering works that have explicitly used the term "digital rhetoric" (or some variant thereof) and then expanding to theories, methods, and practices that implicitly draw on digital rhetoric. In the case of methods, I also look at a range of related fields' approaches that would be available for rearticulation as digital rhetoric methods.

My overall goal is to provide a map of digital rhetoric as an emergent field, focusing on its history, definition, and development as an academic field by looking at the theories that inform digital rhetoric scholarship, the methods used to carry out digital rhetoric research, and the practices that lead to the production of digital texts. I have included not just a review of extant literature (accompanied by critical commentary and a consideration of the contexts and histories of those works) but also my own work, particularly in terms of developing new theories and new methods for working with "born-digital" texts. The book aims to serve as a comprehensive introduction for scholars and students new to the field and for scholars from other fields who find their work intersecting with that of digital rhetoric. I am also making a strong claim for the field identity of digital rhetoric, and I hope it will also serve as a contribution to the field at large as well as promote a visible platform for its continued development. I also suggest that digital rhetoricians have much to offer other fields, such as game studies, human-computer interaction, and Internet studies (as well as close allies such as rhetoric/composition, communication, and media studies), so it may serve as an introduction that digital rhetoricians can recommend to colleagues in other areas as well.

User's Guide

I originally conceived of this project as a traditional (print) text, but through the good fortune of publication by the University of Michigan Press, it has evolved into a dual-natured work, available in both print and digital formats. While a born-digital version of this project would be quite interesting and more interactive, the outcome would be radically different—much of the review of the literature and explication of definitions, theories, and methods presented here simply works better in the traditional academic discursive form. Thus, the differences between the print and digital versions are relatively slight: the online version includes live links and, where appropriate, I have added images, screenshots, and embedded videos (the majority of these are in the final chapter of the book, which focuses on digital rhetoric practice).

Additionally, my hope is that this project is useful for students, scholars, and others interested in digital rhetoric, both in terms of application and identification. I have therefore organized the book into four main parts, each of which focuses on one critical element of digital rhetoric as both field and research methodology. These chapters are independent—that is, they need not be read in order and do not follow a narrative arc or develop a unifying argument over the course of all four sections. Each section of the book also represents a basic overview rather than a comprehensive treatment of all possible theories, methods, or practices; each of the final three chapters also ends with a call to build upon and expand the work presented here.

A Brief Chapter Outline

Chapter 1 provides a **definition** of "digital rhetoric" that distinguishes it from the generalized field of rhetoric and from related areas of concern, chiefly "digital literacy" and "new media." After establishing the working definitions for the book, this first section provides the argument for a view of digital rhetoric as a distinct scholarly field. As an interdisciplinary field, it is tied to the work of several disciplines: rhetoric and writing, composition, technical communication, digital game studies, literacy studies, media (and new media) studies, human-computer interaction, and other interdisciplinary fields such as Internet studies.

Chapter 2 examines **theories** of digital rhetoric (and their relations to classical and contemporary rhetorical theory).

Chapter 3 looks at **research methods** for digital rhetoric, examining current rhetorical and writing studies methods, methods from other fields that might be applied to digital rhetoric research, and a call for the development of new, "born-digital" research methods.

Chapter 4 provides a series of case studies and examples that focus on digital rhetoric as **practice**—in terms of pedagogy, scholarship, and performance.

Future Digital Enhancements

In a future edition of the digital text, I hope to implement a "remix engine"—a system that will allow readers to pull elements from the book, edit them, rearrange them, add additional content, and share the results with others. My programming skills are not quite up to this task as of yet, and I feel that the increased interest in digital rhetoric means that it is more important to provide this overview now and to add additional functionality as soon as I am able.

I welcome suggestions for future editions, and I hope that you will find this text a useful resource.

ONE

Defining and Locating Digital Rhetoric

Because the term "digital rhetoric" appears in a wide range of locations—scholarly articles; in the title of courses offered in departments of communication, English, and writing; academic and popular blogs; discussion lists such as H-DigiRhet; and theses and dissertations in many fields of study—my initial impulse was to resist defining the field of digital rhetoric and instead to follow Sullivan and Porter (1993) and focus on "locating" it with respect to current fields of study. As Sullivan and Porter argue, "defining a concept is a limiting activity; trying to establish a common meaning can have the effect of excluding enriching diversities" (391). This approach, although appropriate for an interdisciplinary field like digital rhetoric, presupposes an established community of researchers and practitioners: in Sullivan and Porter's case, the field of professional writing has a significant body of research and the members of the field had engaged in arguments about how (or whether) it should be defined. Digital rhetoric, in contrast, has not yet become established as a field. An additional consideration is that digital rhetoric draws its theory and methods first and foremost from the tradition of rhetoric itself—and this poses a dilemma because rhetoric is both an analytic method and a heuristic for production, and, critically for our purposes, can be structured as a kind of meta-discipline. The definition of rhetoric is taken up in more detail below, but Kenneth Burke's (1969) commentary on the scope of rhetorical practice is instructive:

> Wherever there is persuasion, there is rhetoric. And wherever there is "meaning," there is "persuasion." Food, eaten and digested, is not rhetorical. But in the meaning of food there is much rhetoric, the meaning being persuasive enough for the idea of food to be used, like the ideas of religion, as a rhetorical device for statesmen. (172–73)

If nearly all human acts of communication engage rhetorical practice (whether explicitly acknowledged or not), then rhetoric-as-method can be applied to all communication events.[1] While I do take a very broad view of the scope of rhetoric, I also believe that articulating a definition of the field provides a focus for future deliberation upon the acceptable methods (derived from the epistemological assumptions underlying such a definition) and practices that may constitute digital rhetoric as a field.

Unlike "rhetoric," a term that has been subject to extensive debate since well before Aristotle published his *Rhetoric* between 336 and 330 BCE, only a few scholars (notably Ian Bogost [2007] and Elizabeth Losh [2009]) have undertaken the task of developing a comprehensive definition of digital rhetoric. The term "digital rhetoric" is perhaps most simply defined as the application of rhetorical theory (as analytic method or heuristic for production) to digital texts and performances. However, this approach is complicated by the question of what constitutes a digital text, and how one defines rhetoric. In the first part of this chapter, I will examine these core terms ("rhetoric," "digital," and "text") and provide an overview and critique of current approaches to defining digital rhetoric. In the second part, I return to the question of location as I examine the relationship between my construction of digital rhetoric and related fields such as digital literacy and new media and other emerging fields such as critical code studies and digital humanities.

Rhetoric

If you are reading a book on digital rhetoric, it is likely that you already have some sense of what rhetoric is and that it has established theories, methods, and practices—along with an extensive number of potential definitions (see Kinney, 2007, for 114 pages of definitions, arranged chronologically from Sappho, circa 600 BCE, to John Ramage, 2006). While it is well beyond the scope of this project to establish a definitive explanation of and definition of rhetoric, it is important to explain the tradition that I draw on and which informs the definition I will advance later in this chapter (and that serves as the starting point for the next chapter, on theories of digital rhetoric).

According to Bizzell and Herzberg (2000), "Rhetoric has a number of overlapping meanings: the practice of oratory; the study of the strategies of effective oratory; the use of language, written or spoken, to inform or persuade; the study of the persuasive effects of language; the study of the relation between language and knowledge; [and] the classification and use of tropes and figures" (1). But, they argue, "Rhetoric is a complex discipline with a long history: It is less helpful to try to define it once and for all than to look at the many definitions it has accumulated over the years and to attempt to understand how each arose and how each still inhabits and shapes the field" (1). And indeed, it is necessary to review the history of rhetoric because our understanding of its use and value depend in part on recognizing and recovering rhetoric from those philosophers and theorists who have sought to minimize its power and/or purview. Contemporary approaches to rhetoric now go far beyond Aristotle's "art of persuasion" in terms of theoretical complexity, but at the same time general usage by the public tends to use the term to mean only style, or worse, as a pejorative applied to false or manipulative arguments.

I will provide more detail about classical and contemporary approaches to rhetorical theory in the next chapter, but the following brief historical overview should provide sufficient context for establishing the framework within which our definition of digital rhetoric will take shape.

Western Classical Rhetoric (Greek and Roman)

One of the earliest definitions of rhetoric is provided by Aristotle in his seminal treatise *On Rhetoric*: rhetoric is "the art (*techne*) of finding out the available means of persuasion" for a given argument (1991, 37). Aristotle goes on to describe how individuals might employ a theoretical framework to discover arguments that might be effective in public deliberation and judgment. Thus, as Richard Buchanan (1989) points out, "rhetoric is both the practice of persuasive communication and a formal art of studying such communication"; moreover, the power of rhetoric's call to persuasion is that it is formulated as an "art of shaping society, changing the course of individuals and communities, and setting patterns for new action" (93).

The practice of rhetoric was originally concerned with the methods one could use to construct a successful persuasive oration; these methods were simplified and codified by Aristotle in the late fourth century BCE. Classical rhetoric was concerned with only three main kinds of speech (and by speech I mean oration, as these methods were developed preliteracy): legal, political, and ceremonial. In constructing a successful speech, the orator could use three modes of expression: logos (logical argument), pathos (emotional ap-

TABLE 1.1

Invention	finding the most persuasive ways to present information and formulate the argument
Arrangement	the organization of the speech
Style	the use of appropriate and forceful language
Memory	using mnemonic devices so you don't forget your lovely style and arrangement
Delivery	presenting the speech effectively (including projection and appropriate gestures)

peals), and ethos (establishing the authority of the speaker). Aristotle divides the process of developing a speech into five stages (the canon of classical rhetoric):

One approach to digital rhetoric has been to map these stages or elements onto practices and examples of digital production (and contemporary attempts to connect the rhetorical cannon to digital texts and performances has lead to revival of theoretical work on memory and delivery—the two elements that appear least applicable to print-text arguments).

Roman rhetoricians (notably Cicero and Quintilian) primarily focused on the political uses of rhetoric (drawing on their Greek predecessors, including Gorgias, Plato, Isocrates, and Aristotle). Quintilian was also interested in the ethical dimension of rhetoric (the "good man speaking well").

Medieval and Renaissance Rhetoric

The rise of Christianity in the medieval period led to the devaluation of rhetoric (it was seen as pagan and antithetical to the church) until Augustine recognized that the persuasive modes of rhetoric could be very useful for the church; however, the focus of rhetoric during this period was primarily in the development of rules for preaching and legal letter writing (all in the service of the church). The study of *style* as the most important rhetorical element gained in popularity, particularly in terms of composing verse.

Rhetoric enjoyed a resurgence of sorts during the Renaissance, although the focus was primarily on style, particularly in terms of defining stylistic elements (a move that was in concert with a general interest in taxonomy in a variety of disciplines). One innovation, however, was the application of rhetoric to private discourse (whereas classical rhetoric concerned itself only with public discourse). In the seventeenth century, two opposing camps of rhetoricians emerged—the Ramists (after Peter Ramus) claimed invention and arrangement for the field of dialectic and limited rhetoric to style, memory, and delivery, while the Ciceronians argued for a classical approach to rhetoric that included the five elements of the canon. In the later part of the Renaissance, Francis Bacon argued that the work of science was inquiry and the work of rhetoric was to serve in support of logic by providing "imagination or impression" (Kiernan 2000, 127)—further divorcing rhetoric from the production of knowledge.

Recovering Rhetoric during the Enlightenment

The focus on style that began in the medieval period and continued unabated through the Renaissance was a sore point for Enlightenment rhetoricians, who worked toward a reformed notion of rhetoric after Locke attacked stylistic ornamentation as an impediment to communication. The call for reform was threefold: rhetoric should rethink its reliance on tropes for invention (and instead focus on observation); syllogistic reasoning should be limited to avoiding fallacies; and clarity should be preferable to ornamental style. The reforms suggested by Bacon and Locke also helped rhetoric ally itself with the new scientific discipline of psychology; this connection led to Bain's "modes of discourse"—modes that mirror the mental processes of description, narration, exposition, argument, and poetry.

Contemporary Approaches to Rhetoric

In the twentieth century, rhetoricians responded to Nietzsche's attack on the quest for objective truth (he argued that knowledge is a social arrangement, rather than an objective entity). I. A. Richards (1930), for instance, argued that meaning is a function of context, and he defines rhetoric broadly as the study of communication and understanding. Kenneth Burke (1966) takes a similarly broad view and considers rhetoric as the study of language as human action that has intentions (motivations) and effects. Burke also considers the ideological function of discourse (connecting people as communities with commonly held beliefs) as an interest of rhetoric.

Chaim Perelman (1982) argues that rhetoric is useful for undermining any claim to any form of knowledge that is absolute (and therefore beyond argument); instead knowledge arises through argument (persuasive rhetoric) within communities that share assumptions and beliefs. Perelman situates the realm of rhetoric as covering the ground between any argument that is not a self-evident truth and arguments that draw persuasive power from coercion or physical force. Bizzell and Herzberg (2001) see contemporary rhetorical theory as focusing on the "source and status of knowledge," and they regard the work of philosophers who consider language and its relation to knowledge (such as Foucault, Bakhtin, Derrida, and Kristeva) as deeply influential to rhetorical theory (14).

The power of rhetoric, as I see it, is that it can be employed as both analytic method and guide for production of persuasive discourse—and it is both of these capacities that inform my understanding of digital rhetoric. Bizzell and Herzberg (2001) provide a definition of rhetoric-as-method, arguing that "rhetoric is synonymous with meaning, for meaning is in use and context, not words themselves. Knowledge and belief are products of persuasion, which seeks to make the arguable seem natural, to turn positions into premises—and it is rhetoric's responsibility to reveal these ideological operations" (14).

I am drawn to this definition because it does not situate rhetorical power within a specific medium of communication (e.g., print or speech); rather it highlights the relationship between rhetoric and knowledge production and meaning-making, not just as a mechanism for persuasion. Similarly focusing on rhetoric as a powerful tool that helps the rhetor produce texts or performances that prompt not just identification but social action, Lloyd Bitzer (1968) argues that "rhetoric is a mode of altering reality, not by the direct application of energy to objects, but by the creation of discourse which changes reality through the mediation of thought and action" (4). While many rhetorical theorists focus primarily on the analytic capacity of rhetoric, it is the value for production that I see as a key resource for the formulation of digital rhetoric.

In a more recent work, Davis and Shadle (2007) consider the value of rhetoric (and pose another fairly expansive definition) as applied to contemporary writing practices:

[I]n a technological age, rhetoric emerges as a conditional method for humanizing the effect of machines and helping humans to direct them. . . . Rhetoric thinks beyond disciplines and "interdisciplinarity"—itself a product of a culture of specialization—by arranging and connecting diverse elements in the pursuit of theoretical questions and practical applications. Rhetoric is a syncretic and generative practice that creates new knowledge by posing questions differently and uncovering connections that have gone unseen. Its creativity does not exclude or bracket history but often comes from recasting traditional forms and commonplaces in new contexts and questions. (103)

But if the definition of rhetoric can be as broad-based as those espoused by Bizzell and Herzberg and Davis and Shadle, why append a prefix to it at all? What distinguishes "digital rhetoric" from the larger expression of "rhetoric" more generally? I would argue that we need to articulate a specific formulation for digital rhetoric for three reasons: at the level of theory, it allows for the use of and alliance with other fields not typically associated with printed text or speech; it prompts a critical view of current rhetorical theories and methods and opens up the question of whether new theories and new methods can or should be developed; and it provides the boundary condition necessary for the emergence of a new field of study.

In the first instance, I see digital rhetoric as similar to visual rhetoric in the sense that a focus outside of the tradition of written and spoken argument broadens the available opportunities to apply rhetorical theory to new objects of study. Visual rhetoric also draws on theory from art and graphic design as well as psychology (gestalt theory), bringing rhetoric into these spheres even as they contribute to the overall rhetorical methods. Because digital rhetoric incorporates the visual (more on this below), it can align itself with these fields, as well as other technical fields—such as computer science, game design, and Internet research—that don't usually take up rhetorical theory or methods. Promoting interdisciplinarity has reciprocal benefits, as each field is enriched through the interaction at the level of theory, method, and practice.

Narrowing the purview of rhetoric to focus on digital texts and performances also highlights the difficulties of applying traditional rhetorical theories and methods to new media compositions and networked spaces. Examining the differences between new forms of digital communication and print text or oral discourse requires us to consider whether we can apply traditional rhetorical methods to these new forms or if new methods and theories may need to be developed. Certainly our traditional notions of "memory" and "delivery" have been complicated and expanded as scholars have attempted to map the canon of classical rhetoric to contemporary digital forms.[2] These approaches are taken up in more detail in the following chapter.

Finally, establishing a specific catalog of theories, methods, and objects of study specific to digital rhetoric allows for the emergence of an interdisciplinary field with a distinct identity—one whose members are drawn from a range of disciplines but who have a shared epistemological foundation. My project here is to provide the beginnings of such a catalog and suggest new areas of development for researchers who identify their scholarly specialization specifically as "digital rhetoric" (as, for instance, faculty who teach digital rhetoric courses and the over five hundred members of the H-DigiRhet discussion list).

While rhetoric provides the primary theory and methods for the field of digital rhetoric, the objects of study must be digital (electronic) compositions rather than speeches or print texts. This is not to say that scholars of digital rhetoric may not make connections between analog and digital objects or focus on the cultural and socio-historical circumstances that lead to, influence, or are imbricated with the construction of digital texts, but that the primary boundary condition for the field is the distinction between analog and digital forms of communication.

Digital

In general usage, "digital" is roughly synonymous with "electronic" or "computerized" and is often used in opposition to its antonym, "analog." In technical terms, digital systems are made up of discrete values whereas analog systems feature a continuous range of values, often represented as a wave (Horak, 2007). As William Pawlett (2007) notes, analog technologies are "based on the principles of similarity, proportion, and resemblance. Digital technologies, by contrast, operate through coded differences rather than proportion or similarity" (79). Although we often use "digital" in reference to computer technologies, any system made up of individual elements satisfies the technical definition: examples of non-computer-based examples of digital systems include writing, Morse code, and the Braille alphabet. Within the context of computer systems and networks, "digital" refers to the encoding of information in binary digits (bits), which may occupy only two distinct states (on or off, 1 or 0).

While the first digital computer, the ENIAC, appeared in 1945, it was Claude Shannon's (1948) "A Mathematical Theory of Communication" that lead the way to our current definition of "digital." In his treatise, Shannon theorized "that the fundamental information content of any message could be represented by a stream of 1s and 0s" (Gaydecki, 13). Digital information streams (encoded as bits) have several distinct advantages over analog signals. Digital data can be more easily replicated in native formats, it can be compressed (thus improving efficiency in transportation of digital information), and it can be made more secure than analog signals.[3] Additionally, analog signals can be digitized (a critical requirement for multimedia production), at which point they can take advantage of the benefits of digital systems. It is this contemporary use of the term and its particular affordances that I invest with the "digital" prefix in "digital rhetoric."

It is important to remember that "digital," however, also has a connection to the material production of texts, whether in print form or electronic. As Angela Haas (DigiRhet.net, 2005) notes

> Digital also refers to our fingers, our digits, one of the primary ways . . . through which we make sense of the world and with which we write into the world. All writing is digital: digitalis in Latin, means "of or relating to the fingers or toes" or "a coding of information." (242)

Haas goes on to argue that historical forms of written communication that were "executed with the use of fingers and codes—from the Mesopotamian Cuneiform, to Egyptian and Mayan hieroglyphs, to Chinese logograms, to Aztec codices"—constitute the "first artifacts of scientific and technological developments, hence the origins of technical communication, visual rhetoric, and digital rhetoric" (243). This stance echoes Lester Faigley's (1998) argument "that literacy has always been a material, multimedia construct" (6) by virtue of the fact that it is, in the strictest sense, digitally constructed. Faigley traces the materiality of literacy from the Mesopotamian clay tokens (dating from the ninth millennium BCE) through the advent of the printing press and concludes that we have only recently become "aware of this multidimensionality and materiality because computer technologies have made it possible for many people to produce and publish multimedia presentations" (6).

In *The Language of New Media*, Lev Manovich (2001) argues against using "digital" as the feature that distinguishes new media from old, declaring the significance of the digital to be a "myth" (52–55). Manovich's technical approach, however, loses sight of the possibilities—the affordances—of digitality; similarly, he does not so much address its constraints per se as to posit that certain aspects of the digital (information loss from analog to digital conversion and identical copies of digital works) break down when examined closely. This kind of specific critique, however, does not consider the power of "digital" as an organizing principle; moreover, my concern here is not so much to focus only on "new media" as objects and products of digital rhetoric as it is to extend the power of rhetoric to digital media and practices—that is, not just digital "arts" but digital communication as well. Borrowing from the appropriation of a physics-based metaphor by Young, Becker, and Pike (1970), I would argue that the power of the digital is in its simultaneous instantiation as both particle and (simulated) wave: digital work (and digitized work) can be articulated and rearticulated, reshaped or recreated as (nearly) perfect copies, carrying with those copies and ancillary works an apparent cohesiveness, but digital work is also composed of discrete bits (individual binary digits)— these components enable reconstruction, but they can also be susceptible to fragmentation. The digital, in other words, is also an apt metaphor for the postmodern, representing both simulacra and fissure.

The digital then, both as a new form of production enabled by information and communication technologies and as a reference to the human history of written communication (from nonalphabetic writing to what we traditionally consider "print"), provides a bridge between textual production (broadly defined to include multimedia) and rhetoric. I would agree with Manovich's (2001) assertion that (print) texts have traditionally "encoded human knowledge and memory, instructed, inspired, convinced, and seduced their readers to adopt new ideas, new ways of interpreting the world, new ideologies"; thus, the printed word (and, I would argue, any material representation of communicative action) has always been "linked to the art of rhetoric" (76–77).

Text

The final element to consider is the notion of digital text—how we choose to define and delimit "text" may circumscribe or open up the objects of study available to digital rhetoric methods. As a student whose early scholarly training was focused solely on literary studies, I initially understood "text" to be a fairly limited term that referenced printed text (and, in particular, literary works); it was not until I began working with cultural studies approaches and postmodern theory that I learned that "any object, collection of objects, or contexts can be 'read' by tracing and retracing the slipping, contradictory network of connections, disconnections, presences, absences, and assemblages that occupy problematic spaces" (Johnson-Eilola 2010, 33). In rhetorical studies, text can be thought of as the container for arguments or persuasive discourse, but that tradition is also usually associated with printed texts (or transcripts of spoken words); for digital rhetoric, we must see text in a far more expansive light.

A good starting point for a broader definition begins with Robert de Beaugrande and Wolfgang Dressler's (1981) approach to "text" as a "communicative event" (1) that meets seven specific criteria of textuality: cohesion, coherence, intentionality, acceptability, informality, situationality, and intertextuality. De Beugrande and Dressler's criteria represent the rhetorical elements of discourse (although they are working in the discipline of linguistics rather than rhetoric). As explained by Titscher et al. (2000),

> *cohesion* represents the structural components of a text: linguistic elements that obey grammatical rules and dependencies
> *coherence* (or textual semantics) constitutes the meaning of a text: "a text creates no sense in itself but only in connection with knowledge of the world and of the text"
> *intentionality* relates to the producer's purpose, thus, "talking in one's sleep would not count as a text, whereas a telephone directory would"
> *acceptability* "is the mirror of intentionality. A text must be recognized as such by recipients in a particular situation"
> *informativity* refers to the quantity of new or expected information in a text
> *situationality* is a way of representing that a given text is context-appropriate (this differs from "rhetorical situation" as it focuses more on "appropriateness" than exigence or response
> *intertextuality* shows that a given text always relates to preceding or simultaneously occurring discourse. (22–23)[4]

This set of criteria maps relatively well to a rhetorical approach to text-as-discourse, although the questions of acceptability and the focus on appropriateness in terms of situation make clear that de Beaugrande and Dressler are concerned only with rhetorically *successful* texts, rather than all texts regardless of the quality of their arguments. Ali Darwish (2008), also working within the field of linguistics, adapts de Beaugrande and Dressler's schema but reframes the elements (which he terms "layers," using digital image production as a metaphor) in more explicitly rhetorical terms. Darwish argues that "text" is comprised of six layers: textual, contextual, cultural, temporal, intentionality, and intertextuality (155–56). Darwish finds the layer metaphor useful because each one can be experienced with varying degrees of transparency, depending on the writer's effective use of rhetoric to connect with the reader; as Darwish argues, "the degree of transparency is determined by the reader's ability to analyze the text and process information and by the shared knowledge and intersubjectivity between writer (as conveyed by the text) and reader" (156).

So, from the field of linguistics we have a consideration of the rhetorical features of text as a representation of discourse. To these criteria, we can draw on semiotics to add the experience of text-as-*designed* discourse. In *Literacy in the New Media Age*, Gunther Kress (2003) proposes a theory of text that includes three categories of text (aesthetically valued, culturally significant, and mundane), each of which is expressly the result of specific design choices:

> text is based, however imperfectly, on the understandings of design: an understanding of what the social and cultural environment is into which my text is to fit, the purposes it is to achieve, the resources of all kinds that I have implement and realize my design, and the awareness of the characteristics of the sites of appearance of that text. (120)

In Kress's formulation, design encompasses a number of rhetorical elements but does not appear to include "audience" as a design consideration except inasmuch as it is embedded within "the social and cultural environment."

Kress also makes two important observations about text. The first is that text is not merely constituted of meaningful symbols but is "the result of social action," which means that literacy "is always seen as a matter of social action and social forces, and all aspects of literacy are seen as deriving from these actions and forces" (86). This syncs nicely with our definition of rhetoric as the means to move the audience into a state of action (often articulated specifically as social action, although it can certainly also be used to prompt individual action). The second point that Kress emphasizes is that "'text' is a material entity, drawing on the resources" of its mode of expression[5] "to realize the significant features of the social environment in which texts were made, shaped, and organized" (87).

Texts have rhetorical features, originate in and propel social action, and are designed material objects; these qualities provide the primary means of relationship between text and rhetoric-as-use. Stephen Mailloux (2002) clarifies this relationship both in terms of rhetoric as analytic method and productive art:

Rhetoric deals with effects of texts, persuasive and tropological. By "texts" I mean objects of interpretive attention, whether speech, writing, non-linguistic practices, or human artifacts of any kind. A production or performance model of rhetoric gives advice to rhetors concerning probable effects on their intended audiences. In contrast . . . a hermeneutic or reception model provides tools for interpreting the rhetorical effects of past or present discourses and other practice and products. (98)

As the definition of text continues to expand to include digital objects that meet the general criteria and associated properties listed above but that also engage a broader range of media, modes, and applications, the analytic capacity of digital rhetoric becomes more likely to provide methods for studying texts that "are not merely *out there*, as objects, but also in motion, gathering other texts around them, responding to their environments in ways both simple and complex, making connections that their authors or readers are participants in" (Johnson-Eilola 2010, 37).

While it is a given that text (like writing) is itself a technology, the affordances of digital production are leading to the development of textual forms that synthesize and enact multiple technologies and media, expanding the notion of text beyond even the fairly broad definitions of discourse-in-material-form presented here. For instance, drawing on Bruce Sterling's (2005) taxonomy of technology types, Johndan Johnson-Eilola (2010) traces the development of text from artifact to product to gizmo to (the as-yet not completely realized) "spime." The key developments in this broader use of "text" that Johnson-Eilola sees for digital rhetoric occur in the articulation of text as "gizmo" and as "spime." Johnson-Eilola argues that "text in the gizmo format represents a dramatic departure from text as product . . . as gizmos, texts are highly unstable and user-alterable in ways that printed texts are not: They can be moved around, recombined, and transformed" (43). The "spime" takes on the qualities of the text-as-gizmo but is also semiautonomous and networked (Johnson-Eilola 2010, 44). Cory Doctorow (2005) sums up Sterling's definition of "spime" as

a location-aware, environment-aware, self-logging, self-documenting, uniquely identified object that flings off data about itself and its environment in great quantities. A universe of Spimes is an informational universe, and it is the use of this information that informs the most exciting part of Sterling's argument (n.p.).

Certainly, texts have what Stan Lindsay (1998), drawing on Burke's theory of entelechy, calls "intrinsic persuasion"—an example particularly germane to digital rhetoric is the case of the website, which persuades each user that it is worthy of use, based on design, usability, and accessibility. But the notion of texts that have a kind of agency (e.g., "spimes")—granted via programming by human actors, but making independent decisions nonetheless)—provides a whole new realm of rhetorical objects that can be theorized and studied using rhetorical methods (see the section on methods for a discussion of traditional and developing methods for digital rhetoric analysis).

Now that we have considered the three main elements that must inform any definition of "digital rhetoric"—rhetoric, digital, and text—we can begin to put them together in pursuit of a suitably expansive definition that both provides an appropriate frame of reference and constitutes the boundaries of the field.

Digital Rhetoric

In October of 1989, Richard Lanham presented a lecture on "Digital Rhetoric: Theory, Practice, and Property"—and this appears to be the first use of the term "digital rhetoric." The lecture was published in *Literacy Online* (Tuman, 1992), and again in Lanham's *The Electronic Word: Democracy, Technology, and the Arts* (1993). Lanham begins by making a connection between computer-mediated communication and rhetoric (placed in opposition to philosophical theories about computing, logic, and artificial intelligence): "in *practice* the computer often turns out to be a *rhetorical* device as well as a logical one, that it derives its aesthetic from philosophy's great historical opposite in Western thought and education, the world of rhetoric" (1992, 221).

Lanham suggests that digital production (and the theories that are brought to bear upon all postmodern production, from psychology, evolutionary biology, sociology, and literary theory) will be called to argue for certain positions within the frame of the law (particularly copyright law), which is "rhetoric's ultimate home" (1992, 242). Beyond questions of law and the move toward democratization through art and theory, Lanham argues that "it is the *computer as fulfillment of social thought* that needs explication" (243, emphasis in original) and that classical rhetoric provides the best theoretical frame for undertaking such an explication.

Lanham's approach focuses primarily on features or properties of digital texts as instantiations of approaches that had arisen previously in artistic and literary forms, rather than positing a fully developed theory or definition of digital rhetoric. However, he does sketch out the important connections between postmodern theory, digital arts, and classical rhetoric and finishes the essay by suggesting that an important next move would be to examine the ethics of digital text.

In *The Electronic Word* (1993), Lanham continues to work out his understanding of the ways in which digital technologies impact the humanities and the role of both technology and rhetoric in higher education, but only in the second chapter (a reprint of the lecture that appeared in *Literacy Online*) does he explicitly evoke "digital rhetoric" as a term of art. One of the drawbacks of this larger collection is that it begins with a chapter that situates his work within literary studies rather than rhetoric, and carries forward this reliance on literary theory, thus implying that digital rhetoric grows out of that subset of rhetorical studies that is the study of literature—rather than the broader and more theoretically robust field of rhetoric as a whole. Lanham thus continues a move that connects digital texts and literary studies, following the lead of the hypertext theorists he cites in his essay (e.g., Barrett, 1988; Bolter, 1991; Landow, 1992).

Early theorists who considered the rhetoric of digital texts focused on hypertext, contrasting hypertextual work with print texts and examining the implications of linking electronic documents in digital networks. While hypertext theory is an important precursor of digital rhetoric, it was fairly limited both in terms of the range of theories used to elucidate what hypertext (ideally) could accomplish and the focus on a fairly narrow construction of hypertext as a specific form. Nonetheless, it is important to gloss this work here, particularly since some contemporary scholars continue to conflate hypertext theory and digital rhetoric.

As with Landow's work, the typical first move in hypertext theory is to connect hypertext to past forms and theories of (print) text. George Landow, editor of *Hyper/Text/Theory* (1994) and author of several influential works on the nature of hypertext contrasts print and digital work thus:

> In contrast to print technology, which foregrounds the physical separateness of each text, hypertext reifies the connections between works and thus presents each work as fundamentally connected to others. Hypertext, in other words, embodies or instantiates Roland Barthes's notions of the individual text as the center of a network. (1991, 71)

He goes on to examine what he sees as the fundamental difference and the place at which new forms of rhetorical activity occur—the hypertext link:

> Electronic linking, which generates the fundamental characteristics of hypertext, changes many of the characteristics of text that derive from print, particularly from the physical isolation of the printed work. By inserting the individual text into a network of other texts, this information medium creates a new kind of textual entity—a metatext or hypermedia corpus. (1991, 71)

Stuart Moulthrop (1994) similarly draws on Barthes in his consideration of hypertext, but he moves beyond the function of the link to create metatexts to considering the geography of hypertext as an enactment of Barthes's "social space of writing." He argues that "[a] rhetorical theory of the contour—augmented, perhaps, by a practical technique of contour representation and navigation—could yield an important shift in our understanding of hypertext. It could allow us to move beyond the concept of the text as a fixed hierarchy (a transformation which collaborative, multi-user hypertexts will demand) while at the same time retaining a sense of the text as an articulated process or object-event" ("Contour and Line").

Like Moulthrop, Doug Brent's "Rhetorics of the Web" (1997) shifts the discussion from the nature of hypertext writing to the question of argumentation in networked hypertexts (specifically looking at the World Wide Web). Brent consciously draws on rhetorical theory and work in literacy studies as opposed to relying primarily on literary theory, which represents an important shift away from "hypertext theory" to "digital rhetoric." He begins by noting that "although hypertext has been used for information retrieval for some time, argument in hypertext is largely a new rhetorical function" (n.p.); he then connects the affordances of digital networks to current theories of rhetoric: "The term 'rhetoric' has expanded well beyond the original meaning of a persuasive argument designed to overpower an audience and bring them over to the speaker's point of view. The 'New Rhetoric' now foregrounds interaction, conversation, and joint construction of knowledge" (n.p.). Brent's invocation of "New Rhetoric" (which comes from Perelman and Olbrechts-Tyteca's work [1969]) is also an important move because the New Rhetoric effectively rescues rhetoric from the Ramistic approach (which limits the purview of rhetoric to "style" or verbal ornamentation) and rejoins it both with the other fields of the classical rhetoric canon and with formal logic.

As digital technologies have continued to develop (at an amazingly brisk pace), the possibilities of constructing hypertext work that includes a variety of media—video, audio, animation, interactive processes—has further marked the departure from our traditional notions of print documents while simultaneously retaining print-based forms within these hypermedia compositions. Thus there has been an increased interest in exploring the possibilities of visual rhetoric(s) as they are foregrounded in digital media. Connecting rhetorical theories of hypertext with visual rhetoric, Gary Heba (1997) suggests the development of a multimedia-based "HyperRhetoric"—"a form of communication that continually invents and reinvents itself through an ongoing negotiation among users, developers, electronic content, and its presentation in a multimedia environment" (22). Heba notes that "from a semiotic perspective, words, images, sounds, textures, smells, tastes, and data markup code in the case of SGML and HTML, are all capable of producing meaningful information. This idea of multisensory communication, the attendant literacies that accompany them, and the technology required to produce and transmit information combine to form the basic condition of HyperRhetoric" (29). One of the more important contributions of Heba's argument, as I see it, is the acknowledgment of infrastructure as a key element of digital rhetoric practice; in this formulation, materiality is not elided for an abstraction (as often happens in early theories of "the virtual").

After 1997, we see a more concentrated turn toward rhetoric, especially on the part of scholars in communications, computers and writing, and composition/rhetoric who are developing and studying computer-based writing pedagogies. One of the most prevalent current practices for making connections between digital media/communications and rhetorical practices is a move to understand "persuasion" in broad terms; Charles Bazerman (1999), for instance, has described persuasion as "the entire range of actions occurring across all discourse networks" (341). And as James Zappen (2005) notes:

> Studies of the new digital media explain some of the basic characteristics of communication in digital spaces and some of their attendant difficulties. Such basic characteristics function as both affordances and constraints and so help to explain how the new media support and enable the transformation of the old rhetoric of persuasion into a new digital rhetoric that encourages self-expression, participation, and creative collaboration. (320)

Similarly, in his discussion of digital images and classical persuasion, Kevin LaGrandeur (2003) suggests that Aristotle's definition is sufficiently broad to cover a great deal of ground, noting that "our 'available means' have expanded considerably" since the original definition was postulated, particularly "with the advent of electronic gadgetry like the computer" (120).

Aristotle also asserts that rhetoric takes up the question of the probable, of subjects that "present us with alternative probabilities" (1357a); this declaration clearly places digital texts under the aegis of rhetoric—for digital works always have the potential of embodying multiple readings; in a sense, they always offer alternative probabilities. Keith Kenney reminds us, too, that classical rhetoric "traditionally was considered to be public, contextual, and contingent" (322), and this is certainly applicable to digital communication: not only does it enact probability in its foundation, but it also functions within contextualizing networks that are typically public and also contingent upon connections to other digital texts (this is particularly apparent in the construction of hypertext as a digital genre).

In *Electric Rhetoric: Classical Rhetoric, Oralism, and a New Literacy*, Kathleen Welch (1999) brings together elements of visual rhetoric and screen literacy, arguing that the humanities—and in particular composition/rhetoric—has neglected to theorize video as a compositional medium that bridges print and oral literacies.[6] Welch begins with a strong argument for the value of classical rhetoric as the basis of analyzing new forms of communication:

> Classical rhetoric as a comprehensive system of discourse theory remains unique among the rhetorical theories available to us because it depends on the relationships among rhetoric, history, politics, educational institutions, and, perhaps most important, the everyday uses of languages that arise from ideological positioning. It treats not only public and private discourse but also the intricate and interdependent relationships between articulation and thought. And it does so in a way that offers powerful alternatives to the normalized way of viewing knowledge in the modern period. (44–45)

The notion that drawing on classical rhetoric can help defamiliarize contemporary approaches is an interesting one, and she uses this approach as leverage to argue for a stronger theorization that "regenders" and "reraces" classical rhetoric at the same time that she deploys it as an interpretive lens for both video and screen. In order to effectively meet both of her goals, she argues that we should not begin with Aristotle, as most other scholars have, but to go back to the Sophists, and to Isocrates in particular:

> by reconstructing Isocrates, we are able to reconstruct classical rhetoric from a series of inert prescriptions (for example, that classical rhetoric is dominantly oral/aural and that writing is peripheral, not influential, or just another convenient tool) and from lists (for example, that classical rhetoric consists of three kinds of speeches, six parts of an oration and so on) into a comprehensive system that depends on weaving articulation and thought, places an emphasis on the production of discourse, and is not confined to the analysis of discourse. (44)

I would argue that contemporary approaches to rhetoric have already reconstructed classical rhetoric into such a comprehensive system, but this approach is part of a larger surge in scholarly interest in the Sophists and a reevaluation of their usefulness for new forms of composition, particularly those at the intersections of visual and verbal rhetorical forms (see, in particular, Covino [1994] and McComskey [2002]). Welch's work features in the history of digital rhetoric because it is arguably the first monograph to fully articulate a theorization of screen-based media via classical rhetoric. The primary drawback is that she focuses primarily on a noninteractive form of video, which lends itself more to analysis than production, and does not extend her argument fully to networked digital computers as tools and media of rhetorical production.

Notwithstanding Welch's attempts to do so, in 2002 Michael Cohen argued that no one had yet successfully articulated a "rhetoric of the digital arts"; that, indeed, for digital texts, there is "nothing like the tradition of classical rhetoric, which, among other things, served to contain, arrange, and codify the choices available to an author" (n.p.). But since the advent of networked, multimedia communication, critics and theorists (some of whom I have cited above) have been struggling to develop a rhetorical theory that can account for multimodal communication, and the advent of digital networks and media has brought forth several attempts to harness the power of rhetoric as both an analytic and a mode of production for creating persuasive communicative works enacted via these new forms of media and distribution. The focal point, however, of Cohen's complaint is the lack of a comprehensive digital rhetoric. While several attempts have been made to construct such a program, most have focused on particular aspects of digital production or the critique of digital works. Zappen (2005) contends that current work toward developing digital rhetoric has thus far resulted in "an amalgam of more-or-less discrete components rather than a complete and integrated theory in its own right. These discrete components nonetheless provide at least a partial outline for such a theory, which has potential to contribute to the larger body of rhetorical theory and criticism" (323).

In "Digital Rhetoric: Toward an Integrated Theory" (in part a follow-up to Zappen, Gurak, & Doheny-Farina's [1997] "Rhetoric, Community, and Cyberspace"), Zappen provides a brief review and synthesis of work that he sees contributing to the establishment of digital rhetoric as an integrated theory,[7] focusing on four major areas:

- the use of rhetorical strategies in production and analysis of digital text
- identifying characteristics, affordances, and constraints of new media
- formation of digital identities
- potential for building social communities (319)

These four elements cover most of the work done by scholars whose work might be categorized as digital rhetoric, and the framework presented here holds up well when considering work published after 2005—and I will return to it as a useful taxonomy (with a few additions) for a more current articulation of the purview and practices of digital rhetoric.

For each element or theme, Zappen reviews the theme presented in three or four works, drawing from a range of disciplines and fields, including communications, literacy studies, sociology, and computers and writing. As I hope will be clear in the next three chapters of this book, digital rhetoric is not tied to a single discipline and, I will suggest, is strengthened by drawing on theories and methods from multiple disciplines and fields while remaining true to its foundation in rhetoric.

Zappen concludes by suggesting that developing "an integrated theory" would offer "new opportunities for inquiry in rhetorical theory and criticism and an expanded vision of what the rhetoric of science and technology might become within the next decade and beyond" (324), but he doesn't offer any suggestions or advice about how to develop such a theory.

Since the publication of "Digital rhetoric: Toward an integrated theory," several scholars have taken up the task of working toward a more coherent and integrated theory. The most detailed approaches appear in the work of Barbara Warnick, Ian Bogost, and Elizabeth Losh (Losh in particular has forwarded the most comprehensive definition/theory to date).

Barbara Warnick's *Rhetoric Online: Persuasion and Politics on the World Wide Web* (2007) was one of the first full monographs to explicitly apply rhetorical theory to the digital texts that reside on the World Wide Web. While Kathleen Welch's (1999) earlier work delved rather deeply into rhetorical theory, her work was directed more at video than digital text; Warnick uses classical rhetoric (from an Aristotelian rather than Sophistic approach) and specifically focuses on political speech presented on the Internet. Warnick begins by invoking Habermas's description of the public sphere and argues that "a good deal of vibrant and effective public discourse in the forms of social activism and resistance occur online, that such discourse has had noticeable effects on society, and that it is therefore worthy of careful study by rhetoricians" (3).

For Warnick, the aim of rhetoric is explicit persuasion and its primary methods for accomplishing this task is through forms of appeal; additionally, the text focuses on analysis through rhetorical criticism and only sketches the value of rhetoric for digital production. Warnick also makes a distinction between rhetoric (forms of appeal), information, and aesthetic elements (which I would call "design" and argue, following Buchanan [1985], are themselves rhetorical elements):

> Rhetorical forms in online media also include coproduced media discourse, online political campaigns and parody, epideictic discourse in online memorials, and other forms of appeal. Often these are hybrid discourses involving information and aesthetic elements as well as rhetoric, but one of their aims will be more or less explicit appeal to purported audiences in specific communication contexts. (13)

Despite (or perhaps because of) these moves to constrain the functions and methods of rhetoric, Warnick provides a solid foundation for the analytic approach of digital rhetoric that is both compelling and quite accessible. Through a series of case studies that examine "the use of the Web for persuasive communication in political campaigns, activist resistance, and other efforts to raise public awareness of major social and political issues" (122), *Rhetoric Online* focuses on three aspects of digital rhetoric: ethos, interactivity, and intertextuality.

Ethos

After establishing her project as the development of a medium-specific approach to the Web as rhetorical space, focusing on "five elements of the communication process—reception, source, message, time, and space" (27), Warnick moves to the first of the three primary aspects of digital rhetoric addressed in the text: ethos.

Ethos is problematic for a rhetorical analysis of Web-based text because the markers of authorship and expertise are often missing or difficult to find; additionally, "the coproduced, distributed communication environment of the Web presents some challenging questions about message credibility" (45).

Drawing on assertions about ethos from Aristotle and Hugh Blair, Warnick points out that "prior to the 18th century, notions of ethos were embedded in the cultural and social mores of host societies" (47) and that ethos was revealed through the argument itself rather than connected to the speaker or writer's qualifications. Indeed, in first year writing courses in most universities, students are taught to investigate the credentials of the speaker as a representation of ethos and examine the argument itself as a form of logos that is not itself directly an appeal to ethos; in this case there is strong support for Warnick's contention that

> [p]reoccupation with the status and expertise of the author has thus moved us away from the idea of ethos as a form of artistic proof in the text and toward the idea of source credibility as an external authorizing mechanism for judging the veracity of what is found in the text. (47)

Warnick proposes an adaptation of Stephen Toulmin's model of field-dependence[8] (cf. Toulmin's [1969] *The Uses of Argument*) as a framework for examining ethos in online texts. Using this approach, "the credibility of an argument is evaluated according to the standards indigenous to the field in which the argument is made"; thus, "users may judge sites according to the procedures, content quality and usefulness, functionality, and values and norms important in the field in which the online site operates" (49). Using *Indymedia* (http://www.indymedia.org) as a case study (chosen in part because many of its contributors are anonymous), Warnick applies a field-dependency analysis to show that the site's readers and contributors "shared values and modes of operation function to enhance the credibility of persuasive messages and arguments posted to the site" (50).

Because her approach focuses on a reception model of media use, Warnick focuses on the ways that ethos may be built for a user community of a particular site but does not extend her analysis to production. And although she notes that users may "rely on a host of factors emerging from a larger system," including "what other sites link to the site in question, whether its content is supported by other content in the knowledge system . . . how well the site functions, and whether it compares favorably with other sites in the same genre" (49), she does not pursue any of these additional methods for developing or analyzing ethos in digital texts.

Interactivity

Following the chapter on ethos, Warnick shifts focus to "interactivity," which she links to Kenneth Burke's articulation of rhetoric as a vehicle for identification, which works particularly well if the object of study is political discourse (as is the case here). Warnick makes a distinction between interactivity as "an attribute of technological functions of the medium, such as hyperlinking, activating media downloads, filling in feedback forms, and playing online games" (69) and user-to-user or text-to-user interaction. Warnick defines interactivity as "communication that includes some form of reciprocal message exchange involving mediation and occurring between [an organization] and users, between users and the site text, or between users and other users," emphasizing "the contingent transmission of messages back and forth as well as text-based interactivity" (75), where the latter "refers to the presence of various stylistic devices, such as use of first person and active versus passive voice," the use of photographs, and other elements that "communicate a sense of engaging presence to site visitors" (73).

This sense of interactivity (particularly the notion of text-based interactivity) seems to me to elide the differences between dialogic communication (reader-to-text and user-to-user interaction) and interactivity as a quality of digital media. As Farkas and Farkas (2002) note, "[c]ontemporary rhetoricians often view texts as dialog. Readers do not just passively receive information; rather, they interact with the text. By contributing their own thoughts and experiences, readers work with authors to create a unique reading experience.

Texts are also dialogic in another sense: To better succeed with their audience, authors instinctively incorporate some of the thinking and attitudes of the audience within their writing" (132). In other words, traditional approaches follow Burke's approach of alignment and identification, but this is not necessarily a function that should be classified as the key property of interactivity.

In the case studies of this chapter, Warnick looks at user-to-user interaction and the opportunities for coproduction of knowledge via websites that facilitate online discussions; contributions of text, image, and video; and organizing tools for face-to-face meetings (the sites in question are moveon.org and georgewbush.com, both of which were analyzed within the context of the 2004 presidential election). In this chapter, Warnick dismisses system-to-user interactivity (which she relegates to functions such as clicking on hyperlinks and customizing site features like font size and image display), noting that she instead "emphasizes forms of interactivity insofar as they function as communication rather than as technologically enabled" (75). This approach is deeply problematic for digital rhetoric, as it essentially argues that the interactive functions of digital systems are a priori arhetorical; this is a limiting move that is similar to characterizing design decisions as outside of the scope of rhetorical analysis (neither of which is a move I can support). A second problem with this approach to "interactivity" is that it constructs it solely through traditional media and therefore privileges a "just apply traditional methods" approach to the analysis rather than considering whether qualities of new media or digital texts should be considered as new forms, perhaps requiring the development of new theory or method.

Intertextuality

In the final section of *Rhetoric Online*, Warnick considers the role of intertextuality in online environments, primarily using political parody and parody advertisements as examples. The goal of the chapter is to identify "strategies used by Web authors drawing upon intertextuality as a resource" and to consider "the probable roles of Web users as readers when they interpret and are influenced by the texts they encounter" (92). Warnick starts with an overview of intertextuality as developed by Kristeva and informed by Bakhtin, which she extends to multimedia compositions (precisely as previous scholars applied the term to hypertext in the late 1980s and 1990s). There doesn't, however, appear to be any real difference in terms of how intertextuality works in practice regardless of online or offline medium; the main conclusion here is that both constructing and, more importantly for Warnick's analysis, understanding texts that use intertextuality as a rhetorical effect is more easily ac-

complished: "contemporary users of Web-based discourse have at their fin-
gertips resources that enable them to seek out information in the moment in
order to more fully understand and appreciate an intertextual reference" (119).

In the end, Warnick argues that because "the nature of Web-based texts
is in many ways very different from that of print texts and monologic speech,
many of the models that have been conventionally used by rhetorical critics and
analysts will need to be adjusted for the Web environment" (121). I would suggest that while this move to "adjust" our theories and methods is perhaps a
necessary first step, it is not a sufficient answer in terms of developing digital
rhetoric as a field—I argue that we need to align theories and methods of classical and contemporary rhetoric to networked texts and new media as objects
of study, but we also need to develop new theories and methods to account for
gaps in these more traditional approaches. One key point that is made in the
conclusion is that there is a significant need for scholars to consider "preservation and a sense of the historical trajectory of the Web's development" (124).
This is still a critical gap for digital rhetoric and Internet studies in general (addressed in more detail in chapter 3, "Digital Rhetoric: Method").

Partly in response to the limitations of the approach that Warnick takes in
Rhetoric Online, Ian Bogost (2007) critiques the notion of "digital rhetoric" as it
had been articulated through 2007, arguing that its "focus on digital communities of practice, treating the computer primarily as a black-box network ap-
pliance, not as an executor of processes" was a significant limitation and that
"digital rhetoric tends to focus on the presentation of traditional materials—
especially text and images—without accounting for the computational under-
pinnings of that presentation" (28).

In *Persuasive Games* (2007), Bogost first calls out a gap in digital rhetoric, arguing that simply applying traditional rhetorical methods are not sufficient for the analysis of new media forms (such as computer games and
simulations):

> Unfortunately, many efforts to unite computers and rhetoric do not even
> make appeals to visual rhetoric, instead remaining firmly planted in the
> traditional frame of verbal and written rhetoric in support of vague no-
> tions of "the digital." *Digital rhetoric* typically abstracts the computer as a
> consideration, focusing on the text and image content a machine might
> host and the communities of practice in which that content is created and
> used. Email, websites, message boards, blogs, and wikis are examples of
> these targets. To be sure, all of these digital forms can function rhetori-
> cally, and they are worthy of study; like visual rhetoricians, digital rhetori-
> cians hope to revise and reinvent rhetorical theory for a new medium. (25)

Bogost further argues that a whole new branch of rhetoric should be established—one that, like visual rhetoric, takes on analytic methods that are specific to the media and forms that are being critiqued. He calls this approach "procedural rhetoric" because it "addresses the unique properties of computation, like procedurality, to found a new rhetorical practice" (26).

Procedurality is not only limited to computer algorithms or video games; as Bogost defines it,

> Procedurality refers to a way of creating, explaining, or understanding processes. And processes define the way things work: the methods, techniques, and logics that drive the operation of systems, from mechanical systems like engines to organizational systems like high schools to conceptual systems like religious faith. (2–3)

For Bogost, however, rhetoric is somewhat simplified relative to the definitions and approaches outlined earlier in this chapter; he simply states that "Rhetoric refers to effective and persuasive expression" (3). I read the focus on "expression" as marking this approach as one that buys into a less robust definition and employment of rhetoric, focusing on the outcomes (reception, via style, as Ramus had suggested) rather than the process (as entailed in invention and arrangement). I would also suggest that the notion of "procedurality" is not absent from contemporary understandings of rhetoric and can be seen as a function even of certain kinds of traditional modes of argument (whether performed in speech, print, or digital forms). For instance, in the introduction to Perelman's *Realm of Rhetoric*, Arnold (1982) notes that "Perelman was led to observe that the acceptability of assumptions about the nature of reality gives some arguments their qualities of rationality; that arguments from example, illustration, and model do not really pretend to be inductions but appear rational by virtue of the 'rules' they imply . . ." (ix).

However, Bogost (2007) makes a compelling case for applying rhetorical principles to a range of digital texts (although the primary—and most compelling—examples are games). He starts by making distinctions among forms of rhetoric based on their application:

> Just as verbal rhetoric is useful for both the orator and the audience, and just as written rhetoric is useful for both the writer and the reader, so procedural rhetoric is useful for both the programmer and the user, the game designer and the player. Procedural rhetoric is a technique for making arguments with computational systems and for unpacking computational arguments others have created. (3)

Bogost's contribution here is important for digital rhetoric, as he identifies an intrinsic quality of digital texts that is not easily or sufficiently addressed by classical rhetorical theory or method (and that is also not directly taken up in accounts of contemporary rhetorical theory or practice). By showing this disconnect between theory and current practice, Bogost reinforces an argument that I will be making in the following sections of this book—namely that digital texts require not just an updating of traditional theory but the development of new rhetorical theories and methods designed to specifically account for the features of digital texts, precisely as Bogost has done here. The majority of *Persuasive Games* makes the case for procedural rhetoric through examples that show how it can be used as a method of analysis (and, as a game designer himself, Bogost also shows how it informs rhetorical production). One of the key values in this approach is the possibility of revealing the underlying structures and ideologies of certain digital texts—a move that is a central practice of contemporary rhetorical criticism.

When Bogost suggests "*procedural rhetoric* is the practice of using processes persuasively, just as verbal rhetoric is the practice of using oratory persuasively and visual rhetoric is the practice of using images persuasively" (28), he presents a method that can and should be taken up by the field of digital rhetoric, just as visual rhetoric itself becomes a method that can be embedded within digital rhetoric research and scholarship.

Bogost's work also clearly influences Elizabeth Losh's take on digital rhetoric (and additional work on persuasive games) as she articulates it in *Virtualpolitik: An Electronic History of Government Media-Making in a Time of War Scandal, Disaster, Miscommunication, and Mistakes* (2009). Losh presents the most detailed and comprehensive definition of digital rhetoric within current literature, and her study should be considered a foundational text for the field. There are, however, some elements with which I disagree, in particular the attempt to connect rhetoric and mathematically based theories from information science (which have proved problematic in the past as well, when similar moves have been made for traditional approaches to oral and print communication). Losh sets up this move by arguing that "in the standard model of digital rhetoric, literary theory is applied to technological phenomena without considering how technological theories could conversely elucidate new media texts" (47); however, I would argue that to this point, there certainly is no "standard model of digital rhetoric" and that the work that has been presented in support of the construction of digital rhetoric draws primarily on the broader panoply of classical and contemporary rhetorical theory (considering in particular the work of Welch and Warnick) rather than the limited subset of rhetorical theory and method as applied in literary studies ("literary theory"[9]). However, I would concede the more important point here—that technological theories (as with Bogost's development of "procedural rhetoric") may well add complexity and depth to the field of digital rhetoric.

At the beginning of her chapter on "Digital Rhetoric," Losh identifies four definitions of digital rhetoric (these definitions are not exclusive, and she aims to demonstrate how they can be woven together to create a more comprehensive approach):

> The conventions of new digital genres that are used for everyday discourse, as well as for special occasions, in average people's lives.
>
> Public rhetoric, often in the form of political messages from government institutions, which is represented or recorded through digital technology and disseminated via electronic distributed networks.
>
> The emerging scholarly discipline concerned with the rhetorical interpretation of computer-generated media as objects of study.
>
> Mathematical theories of communication from the field of information science, many of which attempt to quantify the amount of uncertainty in a given linguistic exchange or the likely paths through which messages travel. (47–48)

The first definition is the broadest, and it generally follows Zappen's (2005) notion that one way to think about digital rhetoric is the employment of rhetorical techniques in digital texts. Losh considers examples of epideictic, deliberative, and forensic categories of rhetoric (from Aristotle's taxonomy) at work in digital spaces and notes that several situations of online persuasion work within multiple categories. Losh argues that "to have basic competence in digital rhetoric also means to understand the conventions of many new digital genres . . . [as] specific and socially regulated forms of digital text that are composed as files of electronic code" (54).[10] Losh moves from describing what I would call approaches to functional digital literacy to showing the connection to the digital rhetoric scholarship: "studying digital rhetoric involves examining ideologies about concepts like 'freedom' or 'honesty' that are in turn shaped by factors like national, linguistic, theological, or disciplinary identity; societal attitudes about ownership and authorship; and cultural categories of gender, race, sexuality, and class" (56) as they are instantiated (and coded into) new digital genres and forms of digital text.

For this first definition, Losh links practices of digital production and performance to classical rhetorical principles such as *kairos* and Aristotle's categories of rhetoric and discusses ways in which classical rhetoric can be applied to digital texts. For instance, she notes that "rhetoricians since the Greeks have acknowledged [the] central position of audience in rhetorical production, but digital dissemination now makes it possible to deliver even more targeted appeals than one would deliver when speaking to an interested crowd of heterogeneous spectators" (59–60), and that "classical rhetoric that focuses on public oratory, the appearance and projection of the speaker, and delivery in indoor or outdoor spaces may be remarkably relevant" (63–64) in digital contexts.

The second is not so much a definition as an example of digital rhetoric analysis in practice, focusing on "the digital rhetoric of the virtual state" (80). This portion of her chapter is similar to the approach taken by Warnick (2007) in the sense that the focus is upon the *uses* of rhetoric in the public sphere. Losh examines "four specific twenty-first-century fields in government rhetoric"—institutional branding, public diplomacy, social marketing, and risk communication. For each of these fields, Losh points out the ways in which digital rhetoric is being employed and how digital affordances and constraints affect rhetorical moves made by governments and large organizations when communicating with a range of audiences. While it is instructive to see where digital rhetoric practices are taking place, I do not see this as part of a definition of digital rhetoric so much as it is an example of an analysis of rhetoric as it plays out in specific digital contexts.

The third definition focuses on digital rhetoric as a field of study, the consideration of which is one of the purposes of this project. Losh notes that "there are faculty appointments advertised for professors of 'digital rhetoric' and courses listed in college catalogs on the subject" (82) as a way of establishing that such a field exists within higher education, and she bolsters the consideration of its constitution as a field by establishing a history that begins in the late 1970s and early 1980s. This history is situated, in part, as an extension of media studies (which connects back to McLuhan), but more so to literary studies. Losh traces the term "digital rhetoric" to Lanham's (1992) essay but also draws connections to the work of hypertext theory and to the incorporation of poststructuralist critical theory by scholars such as Landow and Ulmer. Losh's reading of Lanham also contextualizes it as a response to current debates in literary studies about the "death of print":

> In formulating a disciplinary realm for digital rhetoric, Lanham appeases the traditionalists by attempting to integrate new media studies into a longer rhetorical history. Yet, at the same time, he is alerting his colleagues that a fundamental paradigm shift is taking place in the present moment. . . . In his work on the "sociality of knowledge," Lanham argues that "electronic information" not only changes what is meant by "author" and "text," but also "desubstantializes" the arts and letters, along with the industrial revolution that produced them. (84)[11]

This focus on digital literary studies and hypertext theory is certainly an important part of the history of digital rhetoric, but I would suggest that it leaves out the work of composition/rhetoric scholars who were focused on digital rhetoric as productive method and as practice (as opposed to a narrower focus on digital rhetoric as analysis and critique). There are also scholars in media studies and communications who were exploring the possibilities presented by what they called "information-communication technologies," or ICTs, as transformative processes in fields such as technical communication and education. Thus, while Losh rightly asserts that "the objects of study in much new media scholarship are not very relevant to the political interests of the public at large" such as "[a]rt installations in small galleries, hypertext novels with cult followings, and procedural poems by poets considered too minor to be represented in chain bookstores" (88), I would argue that these are not, in fact, the objects of study of digital rhetoric *per se* but historical precursors from fields that lead to and inform—but do not constitute—digital rhetoric.

In terms of field development, Losh "sees two possible shortcomings to the bulk of critical work done in digital rhetoric to date: marked tendencies to overlook the rhetoric of the virtual state and to ignore theories about rhetoric from the discipline of computer science" (88). The first of these critiques is answered by her own work in *Virtualpolitik*. And depending on where one draws the boundaries and participants in digital rhetoric, it is possible to find work from scholars in public policy that explicitly consider the virtual state (a term Losh draws from Fountain, 2001) in rhetorical terms (see, for instance, Garson's [2006] *Public Information Technology and E-governance: Managing the Virtual State* and Fountain's [2001] *Building the Virtual State: Information Technology and Institutional Change*).

I find the second critique somewhat more problematic. Losh argues that "despite appeals to those with interdisciplinary credentials, [work in digital rhetoric] often excludes highly relevant literature from technologists who may have a more intimate understanding of the systemic constraints that govern the representation, processing, or retrieval of information that may be central to communicative exchanges effected through digital media," and she also claims that "a basic understanding of both signal theory and network theory is valuable to any contemporary rhetorician" (89). While it is likely that network theory is certainly useful (and, indeed, many more recent works in digital rhetoric and related fields have appropriated theories and methods from network theory, e.g., Rice, 2006; Nakamura, 2008; van Dijk, 2009), prior attempts to synthesize communication theory (meaning the mathematical principles of information encoding and decoding via telecommunications systems) and rhetorical theory have been less than successful.

With regard to the value of formal mathematical theory, I will begin by noting that Perelman and Olbrechts-Tyteca's (1969) evaluation of a great number of argumentative strategies from real-life situations shows that formal logic does not in fact play a role in developing successful argument (in part because it aims for an answer that is certain rather than one that is provisional). They showed that strategies of formal logic and quantification clearly did not belong within the realm of rhetoric at all when it came to the actual practice of rhetorical argumentation.

But the specific information transference model that Losh draws upon (the Shannon-Weaver model) had long been in use as a model of practice for technical communication—with the undesirable effect of treating people whose task it was to help convey information from subject matter experts to lay audiences as mere automata who were instructed to eliminate "noise" in the signal that moved from expert to user. When put into use, this model led to an extremely deficient construction of the value and use of the technical communicator, and it wasn't until it became clear that technical communicators could contribute to projects at the stage of invention (particularly the production of digital texts), which was put forth in terms of user-centered design, that the damage done by this model began to be reversed. Slack, Miller, and Doak (1993) forcefully argued against the model of technical communicator-as-transmitter, instead positing that rhetoricians in the field of technical communication should be seen as both translators of information and as articulators (in the Stuart Hall sense) within the communication network. Slack, Miller, and Doak described the communication theory based on the Shannon-Weaver model as the transmission view of communication because it was developed as a technological schema for transmitting a message from one point to another using telecommunication devices.

Shannon's work (published with Warren Weaver as *A Mathematical Theory of Communication* in 1949) argued that "the fundamental problem of communication is that of reproducing at one point either exactly or approximately a message selected at another point" (1). In this transmission view, there is no need for rhetoric, as persuasion is not part of the model. In fact, *meaning is not a part of the model* either, as the focus is the transmission of a message (as information) regardless of content. Gilbert Simondon (1989), who calls this a technical theory of communication, makes the fairly obvious critique that a model that sees only a single channel of transmission between only two points must necessarily eliminate most of the complexity of actual human communication.

In *Network Culture: Politics for the Information Age*, Tiziana Terranova (2004) attempts to directly take up Shannon's model (and other elements of information theory that came after) to not only inform an approach to digital rhetoric but to serve essentially as a replacement for rhetoric itself—to provide an ana-lytic method that addresses communication not from a rhetorical standpoint but through an information theory lens. While many of the later chapters in this text do provide useful approaches to developing new theories for digital rhetoric, the first chapter (wherein she introduces the Shannon-Weaver model and argues that it can be read in ways that provide a new way of consider-ing digital communication) ultimately leads to a rephrasing of rhetoric, but in technical terms. When Terranova states that

> information is neither simply a physical domain nor a social construc-tion nor the content of a communication act, nor an immaterial entity set to take over the real, but a specific reorientation of forms of power *and* modes of resistance. On the one hand, it is about a resistance to in-formational forms of power as they involve techniques of manipulation and containment of the virtuality of the social; and on the other hand, it implies a collective engagement with the potential of such informational flows as they displace culture ad help us to see it as the site of a *reinvention* of life (37),

I would suggest that this description could just as easily refer to rhetoric itself (and digital rhetoric in particular, as it is applied to information flows).

Thus, while I do think that some contemporary approaches to informa-tion science are valuable contributors to the work of the digital rhetorician (particularly in terms of the development of *methods* that can be used within the practice of digital rhetoric[12]), I would reject the argument that the math-ematical approach of "technical" communication theory is in any way a useful departure.

A Note on Competing Terms

Before examining digital rhetoric's relationship to and position within a net-work of related fields and activities, I want to make a brief digression to ex-amine the relatively few alternative titles that have been suggested by others who are interested in digital rhetoric—but who elect to call it by a different name. There are many examples of terms like "online rhetoric" and "network rhetoric" that appear in a wide range of scholarly literature, but in most cases these use "rhetoric" to refer to choices made by individuals or groups who are promoting a particular argument or ideology rather than as rhetorical theory or method established in online milieu or networked systems. The three main alternative terms that have been suggested are "electric rhetoric," "computa-tional rhetoric," and "technorhetoric."

Electric Rhetoric

Although Welch (1999) used "Electric Rhetoric" as the title of her monograph, its use as a descriptive term for rhetorical analysis of electronic texts did not see much widespread use. Perhaps "electric" is too broad a term; I also believe that electric is tied distinctly to the physical properties and infrastructure of digital text—and while it is important to acknowledge the connection between the digital and the material, the term itself is, I think, a bit too concrete. Another possibility is that Welch's definition itself is too limiting, since she never moves beyond print literacy: "Electric rhetoric, an emergent consciousness or mentalité within discourse communities, is the new merger of the written and the oral, both now newly empowered and reconstructed by electricity and both dependent on print literacy. Electronic technologies have led to electronic consciousness, an awareness . . . that now changes literacy but in no way diminishes it" (104). While Welch's work is pioneering and valuable to digital rhetoric for its approach, I would argue that we need to move beyond only considering orality and print as the dominant literacies available to digital rhetoricians.

Computational Rhetoric

A more recent trend has been to argue that the humanities have neglected the possibilities of computation as a method and that we could develop a "computational rhetoric" that would bridge qualitative and quantitative/algorithmic approaches to humanities research. Some of the main proponents of this term also use methods from computational linguistics, but they use them in the pursuit of rhetorical analyses (see, for instance, Michael Wojcik's [2011] work on sentiment analysis in student writing). This new call for the construction of a computational rhetoric echoes approaches from computer science's subfield of artificial intelligence called argument and computation (which relies on the development of argumentation schema and computational methods for addressing and processing informal logic and persuasion). Floriana Grasso's (2002) "Toward a Computational Rhetoric" and "Computational Models of Rhetorical Argument," by Crosswhite et al. (2004) are good examples of attempts to use rhetoric to inform the programming of artificial intelligence systems. The main drawback to this approach, and to the current call for its uptake in the humanities and in computers and writing in particular, is its reliance on formal argumentation schema—this is rhetoric-as-argument only, which is as reductive as rhetoric-as-ornamentation, but in the opposite direction. Another issue is the difficulty of representing complex systems purely algorithmically (in a way, computational rhetoric faces the same challenges as attempts to draw on quantitative modeling from information science that I've outlined above). And, contrary to Bogost's assertion that "'digital' gets the materiality of computation wrong" (n.p.), I believe that it is far easier to elide material connections when focusing on computation, which does not have strong and distinct connections to the material in its lineage and etymology in the way that "digital" does.

Computational rhetoric as a model for integrating methods from computer science, linguistics, and rhetoric does have much to offer as a facet of digital rhetoric (and I would suggest that some of the issues that arise within computational rhetoric, such as the consideration of whether nonhuman agents can engage in rhetorical communication[13] is an important question for digital rhetoric as well).

Technorhetoric

The term technorhetoric (or techno-rhetoric) and the related scholarly identity of technorhetorician gained popularity in the computers and writing field in the late 1980s, promoted as a term that evoked both an interest in rhetorics *of* technology and rhetoric *as* technology (in the sense that it is rooted in techne).[14] As Keith Dorwick (2005) explains it, "the distinction between being a technorhetorician and a rhetorician is a difference of subject matter only: The rhetorics of technology certainly have their own scholarly material . . . but the techniques, the ways of reading the material, are quite similar throughout the entire field. . . . In our subdiscipline, then, we study technology and perhaps most especially in our classrooms, but we are always rhetoricians when we do so" (92, n. 1). More recently, Jimmie Killingsworth (2010) has provided a more formalized definition, calling it "the study, practice, and teaching of electronic literacies, as in the fields of new media studies and computers and composition" (77).

While "technorhetoric" as a portmanteau of "technology" and "rhetoric" works relatively well as a descriptor of the interests and practices of digital rhetoric (and I have used it myself in the past), it doesn't seem to have enjoyed the kind of cross-disciplinary uptake that "digital rhetoric" has seen. For my purposes, I see the use of the term as roughly synonymous with "digital rhetoric" (and would more likely describe myself as a technorhetorician—at least in less formal contexts—than I would call myself a digital rhetorician).

Digital Rhetoric: A Definition

Although I believe that digital rhetoric as a field designation provides opportunities for developing new theories, methods, and practices (and is thus not just a difference of subject matter), Dorwick's point that we approach the questions we are interested in as rhetoricians is really the key element in defining digital rhetoric. In the end, I return to the definition with which I started, but now carrying a richer understanding of the key terms—rhetoric, digital, and text—that feature in that definition:

The term "digital rhetoric" is perhaps most simply defined as the application of rhetorical theory (as analytic method or heuristic for production) to digital texts and performances.

I would add, following Zappen (2005), that the primary activities within the field of digital rhetoric include

- the use of rhetorical strategies in production and analysis of digital text
- identifying characteristics, affordances, and constraints of new media
- formation of digital identities
- potential for building social communities (319)

but I would add to that list

- inquiry and development of rhetorics *of* technology
- the use of rhetorical methods for uncovering and interrogating ideologies and cultural formation in digital work
- an examination of the rhetorical function of networks
- theorization of agency when interlocutors are as likely to be software agents (or "spimes") as they are human actors

Finally, I would note that digital rhetoric may use any of the rhetorical fields and methods that may be useful in any given inquiry, including those of traditional/classical rhetoric, contemporary theories of rhetoric, visual rhetoric, computational rhetoric, and procedural rhetoric—and that as an interdisciplinary field, it may also avail itself of methods drawn from a wide range of related disciplines.

Digital Rhetoric and . . .

In addition to explicating a definition of digital rhetoric by examining the terms that make up the definition, the way that digital rhetoric functions via theory, method, and practice, the ways in which it constructs itself as a field of inquiry, and the history of the theories, fields, methods, and approaches that have led to our current understanding of the term, it is important also to situate the field within the network of related fields and activities. Following Sullivan and Porter (1993), I believe that "describing the field in terms of a general terrain encompassing several different spheres of activity can maintain a dynamic pluralism and promote an interdisciplinary character" (391–92), which is certainly one of the goals of the present project.

I have selected a number of fields that are closely connected to or inform digital rhetoric (there are others, and a more comprehensive network map of these fields and their interrelationships is the aim of a future project, but the ones I have selected play key roles in my understanding of how digital rhetoric functions as an emerging field in its own right). The fields that I address here are:

Digital literacy (articulated as a requirement of digital rhetoric)
Visual rhetoric (which provides a range of necessary methods)
New media (as the object of study of digital rhetoric)
Human-computer interaction (a related, well-established field)
Critical code studies (a related, emerging field)

I will complete my inventory with an overview of the relationship of digital rhetoric to two broad interdisciplinary approaches in the humanities and social sciences (respectively): digital humanities and Internet studies.

Digital Literacy

Digital literacy is a requirement of digital rhetoric—that is, just as print literacy is necessary for a writer to deploy traditional rhetorical moves, the same is true of digital writing practices. Digital literacy is more complex in some ways because it requires the user to be able to read and write with a number of sign systems (e.g., coded web pages, video, audio, image, animation), each of which has its own functional and critical requirements. The question for digital rhetoric, however, is one of relationships: how do we define digital literacy (in both functional and critical terms) and how does it impact the field of digital rhetoric?

Various scholars have spoken of computer literacy, media literacy, electronic literacy, or silicon literacy in attempts to identify communicative technology use as a valid domain for literacy instruction; however, others have rejected the coupling of these modifiers with the term "literacy" as it serves to dilute our understanding of (print) literacy. In *Literacy in the New Media Age*, Kress (2003) argues that "*literacy* is the term to use when we make messages using letters as the means of recording that message . . . my approach leaves us with the problem of finding new terms for the uses of the different resources: not therefore 'visual *literacy*' for the use of image; not 'gestural *literacy*' for the use of gesture; and also not musical '*literacy*' or 'soundtrack *literacy*' for the use of sound other than speech; and so on" (23). Kress very specifically differentiates literacy as oriented to writing, although he acknowledges that computer technologies problematize this artificial distinction between modes. It appears that Kress seeks to make a distinction between resource (knowing how to write) and use:

> *Literacy* remains the term which refers to (the knowledge of) the use of the resource of writing. The combination of knowledge of the resource with knowledge of production and perhaps with that of dissemination would have a different name. That separates, what to me is essential, the *sense of what the resource is* and what its potentials are, from associated questions such as those of its *uses*, and the issue of whatever skills are involved in using a resource in wider communicational frames. (24)

While this distinction may be useful for the construction of his social-semiotic theories of language use, it seems to me that separating the resource from the production (use) and dissemination is to decontextualize literacies by disembedding them from their social, historical, and cultural milieu; moreover, by limiting "literacy" to "writing with letters" (61), one is forced to separate the written from the visual, despite the inherently visual nature of writing. If we agree that literacy is rooted in sociohistorical contexts (Street, 1984), it must encompass more than the particular sign system of writing with letters. And although literacy itself is multimodal, it is useful to differentiate the particular modes or uses of literacy when seeking to observe the effects of literacy practices; thus, rather than seeking a different name for meaning production that includes more than just writing, I would prefer to couple the concept of literacy as sociohistorically situated practice with a modifier that allows us to make a distinction between those practices that are culturally located within print media and those located within digital media.

In *Teletheory* (1998), Gregory Ulmer argues that "[w]e need a new genre that will give us better access to the thought that video has already given us to think, if not to represent in alphabetic writing" (xii); like Welch, Ulmer focuses here on the image (and video in particular), but his overall body of work has expanded to include the full range of digital media.[15] He suggests "electracy" as the designation for digital literacy; however, his approach is more complex in that he focuses not on literate practice but on literacy as apparatus: "An apparatus is not only a technology (e.g., the alphabet, paper, ink etc.) but also an institution and its practices developed along with the technology" (Memmott 2000, 1). In an interview with Talan Memmott (2000), Ulmer explains that

> "Electracy" is a neologism, then, to give a name to the apparatus of the emerging digital epoch . . . it helps us see the difference between "media lit-

eracy" (whose goal is to protect from or defend against electracy by means of forms and practices specific to the previous apparatus; the equivalent for an oral person calling literacy "alphabetic orality"). It also is generative in that, knowing by analogy with literacy that digital technological shift is just one part of an apparatus, we may notice that the other parts of the apparatus shift are also well under way—for example that a new institution has emerged within which is being invented the set of practices that will be to electracy what schooling and all that goes with it are to literacy. (1)

While electracy is a useful concept for digital rhetoric, its function as an apparatus (as Ulmer sees it) sets it apart from an understanding of literacy as defined within literacy studies and as I use it here. Unlike digital literacy, electracy is more of a method than a condition, and as such is not a *requirement* for digital rhetoric so much as it is a potential tool.

Selfe and Hawisher (2004) use the term "literacies of technology" "as an all-encompassing phrase to connect social practices, people, technology, values, and literate activity, which, in turn, are embedded in a larger cultural ecology" (2); while I would agree that the term we use should include all of those elements, I see "literacies of technology" as parallel to "rhetorics of technology"—that is, an analysis of how technologies are articulated by those who write about and construct them. The term also implies that technology takes on the values of literacy for itself, which to me evokes Feenberg's (1999) critique of technological determinism (that is, that "decontextualized, self-generating technology" acts "as the foundation of modern life" [78]).

I prefer the term "digital literacy" because I believe it captures the notion that the literacy practices referred to are enacted in digital spaces—I would contrast this sense of media, location, and context with terms such as "computer literacy," which evokes a concept of mere tool use, "internet literacy," which is too specific both in locale and in historical moment, and "electronic literacy," which is too broad in scope (as it can be seen as referencing any electronic device). "Technological literacy" or "technology literacy" is similarly too broad, as nearly all modes of communication are technologies—so there is no functional distinction between print-based literacy and digital literacy.

However, digital literacy also goes beyond the textual and includes the effective use of symbolic systems, visual representations of language, and digital object manipulation. Snyder (2002) argues that, "in an electronically mediated world, being literate is to do with understanding how the different modalities are combined in complex ways to create meaning. People have to learn to make sense of the iconic systems evident in computer displays—with all the combinations of signs, symbols, pictures, words and sounds" (3). Carmen Luke (2000) frames her articulation of digital literacy practices via the notion of "multiliteracies":

> Meaning-making from the multiple linguistic, audio, and symbolic visual graphics of hypertext means that the cyberspace navigator must draw on a range of knowledges about traditional and newly blended genres or representational conventions, cultural and symbolic codes, as well as linguistically coded and software-driven meanings. (73)

The notion of multiple forms of literacy—of multiliteracies—also informs the way that Selfe and Hawisher (2004) describe the focus of their work in *Literate Lives in the Information Age*: "As the title of our book attests, however, we endorse linking literacy with words, such as *technological, digital, electronic*, as well as the all encompassing *literacies of technology*. We believe that by naming these abilities *literacies*, we signal the enormous importance they hold for functioning in today's literate world" (1). One of the key elements of Selfe and Hawisher's approach is that they make clear that their use of the term literacy specifically connects to "communication skills and values—rather than on the skills required to use a computer" (2), thus providing a distinction from the general usage of "computer literacy" as an indication of technological savvy or ability to use specific computer programs and tools. I would suggest, however, that computer literacy is a necessary and embedded component of digital literacy and would be an appropriate name for the functional digital literacy necessary for the development of critical digital literacy and for the use of digital rhetoric.

The definition of "21st century literacies" provided by the National Council of Teachers of English (2008) also takes a multiliteracies approach that situates literate practice as more than just skill-based:

> Literacy has always been a collection of cultural and communicative practices shared among members of particular groups. As society and technology change, so does literacy. Because technology has increased the intensity and complexity of literate environments, the twenty-first century demands that a literate person possess a wide range of abilities and competencies, many literacies. These literacies—from reading online newspapers to participating in virtual classrooms—are multiple, dynamic, and malleable. As in the past, they are inextricably linked with particular histories, life possibilities and social trajectories of individuals and groups. (n.p.)

This definition helpfully includes both computer literacy (skills for using the tools of technology) and the wider critical concerns, as well as pedagogical learning objectives. It is this definition that I will be using when I employ the term "digital literacy" as a requirement of both students and scholars of digital rhetoric.

Visual Rhetoric

While digital literacy is a requirement for using digital rhetoric (either analytically or as a framework for composition), visual rhetoric is an example of a discrete set of methods and theories that are available to use within the digital rhetoric context. At the same time, visual rhetoric parallels digital rhetoric in the sense that it too draws on a number of different fields and disciplines and uses rhetoric as the common theoretical foundation.

In *Defining Visual Rhetorics*, Charles Hill and Marguerite Helmers (2004) address the difficulty of establishing a singular definition, noting that even within the community of rhetoricians who claimed the visual as their object of study,

> there seemed to be very little agreement on the basic nature of the two terms visual and rhetoric. To some, studying the "visual" seemed to consist solely of analyzing representational images, while to others, it could include the study of the visual aspect of pretty much anything created by human hands—a building, a toaster, a written document, an article of clothing—making the study of "visual rhetoric" overlap greatly with the study of design. To still others, the study of visual rhetoric seemed to necessarily involve a study of the process of looking, "the gaze," with all of the psychological and cultural implications that have become wrapped within that term. (ix)

Unlike digital rhetoric, visual rhetoric has a longer history (although the question of definition has remained less than concrete throughout). An oft-cited work that serves as a touchstone for the turn to the visual in rhetorical studies is Roland Barthes's (1977) "The Rhetoric of the Image," wherein he examines the question of where meaning resides in the image and how we might analyze it using a semiotic approach. Barthes asserts that images function both connotatively and denotatively, and that the connotative signifiers form a rhetoric that serves as the signifying aspect of ideology (49). The rhetoric of the image, he suggests, is subject to physical constraints but that its meaning can be read (at least in part) through a rhetorical analysis of the formal relations of the visual elements that comprise it (50). As Carolyn Handa (2004) points out, "one of Barthes' fundamental points is that in the vast majority of cases, cultures work hard to assure that images to not simply connote, but are clearly anchored, 'denoted' either by verbal text or cultural context, so that their connotative powers do not exert unpredictable effects on their audiences" (134). It is the question of audience and the image's persuasive effect (rather than simply aesthetic effect) that serves as one of the foundational elements of visual rhetoric. In "Images in Advertising: The Need for a Theory of Visual Rhetoric," Linda Scott (1994) provides a literature review that draws on the visual arts, anthropology, and the psychology of pictorial perception in an examination of historical and theoretical approaches to the nature of the image, ultimately arguing (along similar lines as Barthes, although coming from a different perspective) "that images are not merely analogues to visual perception but symbolic artifacts constructed from the conventions of a particular culture" (252).

And, also like digital rhetoric, visual rhetoric functions both as a practice and as a field of study. As Sonja Foss (2004) notes, visual rhetoric can refer both to a visual artifact and to a perspective on the study of visual data: "In the first sense, visual rhetoric is a product individuals create as they use visual symbols for the purpose of communicating. In the second, it is a perspective scholars apply that focuses on the symbolic processes by which visual artifacts perform communication" (304).

Visual rhetoric appears alongside digital rhetoric in a number of contexts, and there are many examples of the use of visual rhetoric methods for digital rhetoric projects. In "Understanding Visual Rhetoric in Digital Writing Environments," Mary Hocks (2003) explicitly connects visual and digital rhetorics and suggests that "because modern information technologies construct meaning as simultaneously verbal, visual, and interactive hybrids, digital rhetoric simply assumes the use of visual rhetoric as well as other modalities" (631). Examples of uses of visual rhetoric in digital rhetoric scholarship range from fairly traditional examinations of visual objects represented digitally to considerations of web and software interface design, to the decoration of the physical objects we use to access online information and carry out digital communications. Paul Heilker and Jason King's (2010) review of the use of visual rhetoric by online autism communities, focusing on the debates about the design of a visual symbol, which shifted from ribbon to puzzle to closed infinity symbol, is a recent example of embedding traditional visual rhetoric analysis within online research (121–22). Visual rhetoric is often invoked in digital rhetoric studies when examining website interfaces, as in Johndan Johnson-Eilola's (2008) extensive use of search engine screenshots, or in the examination of the interfaces of digital composing tools, such as Sean William's (2008) exploration of the process of simulation in Dreamweaver. Considerations of visual rhetoric also extend beyond the screen, as Meredith Zoetewey's (2010) work on "expanding wireless research to include mobile devices' exteriors" (138) in an effort to redefine laptops as objects of inscription by examining the visual choices and ornamentation that users apply to their mobile computers.

A complication for the use of visual rhetoric in a digital rhetoric context is the conflict that arises when the methods of production and analysis are insufficient to fully engage new media. Ian Bogost (2007) has argued that while "there is much value to be gained from the study of images in all media . . . in procedural media like videogames, images are frequently constructed, selected, or sequenced in code, making the stock tools of visual rhetoric inadequate. Image is subordinate to process" (23–24). Thus, while visual rhetoric and digital rhetoric are often intertwined and are closely related in a number of ways, it is clear that visual rhetoric's methods address only one aspect of digital rhetoric analysis and production.

New Media

Like digital rhetoric (and visual rhetoric), the term "new media" has been the subject of competing interpretations and definitions. Most approaches consider new media a description of a particular kind of object (or text, using the expansive definition of that term), although there has also been some attempt to use new media as a kind of self-reflexive term for the study of new media objects as well. One of the difficulties with the term is that it doesn't have clear referents to prior fields (at least, not directly, as "media" is not the equivalent of "media studies") and both elements have been contested: when do particular media stop being "new"? And are the "media" of "new media" necessarily or obviously digital? Thus, I begin this brief overview of new media with the caveat that the definitions I have chosen to draw on are both contemporary and contingent and that I agree with Packer and Jordan's (2001) assessment that

> Digital media's peculiar nature challenges traditional categories; this in itself is an aspect of its radical character. But there is value in proposing and discussing alternative definitions of digital media—even if these definitions are contingent, bracketed by circumstances. In fact, it may be best to regard them as contingent, because our experience with digital media is so fresh, and where it leads so unclear. The definitions of today will inevitably be replaced tomorrow, as new applications for digital media emerge over time. (xxxii)

Some approaches treat new media as equivalent to multimedia. Cynthia Selfe (2004) defines "new media" as "texts created primarily in digital environments, composed in multiple media (e.g., film, video, audio, among others), and designed for presentation and exchange in digital venues" (43). This definition follows the same trajectory as Randall Packer and Ken Jordan's (2001) description of multimedia: "while not all computer-based media is multimedia, today's multimedia starts with the computer, and takes the greatest advantage of the computer's capability for personal expression" (xvii). Two of the key elements of multimedia shared by new media are the mixing of media and the requirement for users of both forms to engage multiple literacies (thus, as for digital rhetoric, digital literacy is a requirement of new media use and production). Selfe (2004), arguing for new media as a form of writing that should be taught in composition courses and curricula, describes the relationship between new media as text and traditional print by pointing out that "although such texts often include some alphabetic features, they also typically resist containment by alphabetic systems, demanding the multiple literacies of seeing and listening and manipulating, as well as those of writing and reading" (43).

In *Remediation: Understanding New Media* (1999), Jay Bolter and Richard Grusin focus not on defining new media based on unique features or the affordances of digital (re)production but instead examine how new media reshape and reconfigure "old" media when they are drawn into the mix and play of new media composing. Their work, like others that follow, considers new media in larger historical and cultural contexts, which is (in part) an extension of (not-new) media studies approaches. Bolter and Grusin suggest that new media must be defined through its relationship with older media:

> No medium today, and certainly no single media event, seems to do its cultural work in isolation from other media, any more than it works in isolation from other social and economic forces. What is new about new media comes from the particular ways in which they refashion older media and the ways in which they refashion older media and the ways in which older media refashion themselves to answer the challenges of new media. (15)

Perhaps the most comprehensive approach to defining new media is Lev Manovich's influential *The Language of New Media* (2001). Manovich draws on the histories of art, photography, video, telecommunication, design, and cinema to develop his theory and definition of new media (although he does draw on literary theory, rhetoric is otherwise absent from his consideration). In his articulation of new media as cultural object, he both includes and expands Bolter and Grusin's notion that new media draw upon and reshape older media, claiming that "new media objects are cultural objects; thus, any new media object—whether a Web site, computer game, or digital image—can be said to represent, as well as help construct, some outside referent: a physically existing object, historical information presented in other documents, a system of categories currently employed by culture as a whole or by particular social groups" (15).

Manovich argues that what separates new media from other media is that the underlying structure of all new media is computer-accessible numerical data. For Manovich, "the translation of all existing media into numerical data accessible through computers" is the foundation of new media, which is composed of "graphics, moving images, sounds, shapes, spaces, and texts that have become computable; that is, they comprise simply another set of computer data" (20). From this premise, Manovich proposes five principles of new media: numerical representation, modularity, automation, variability, and transcoding. These are not so much features of new media that can be identified as they are formations that work on new media objects and whose effects are embedded within but not always immediately identifiable as contributing to the new media composition itself. The explication of these principles and their application as a test for delineating new media from other media forms serves as a methodological framework; ultimately, Manovich provides a rhetorical method[16] for constructing and elucidating new media texts. The basic functions of these five principles are:

Numerical Representation. New media are composed of digital code and thus subject to algorithmic manipulation; that is, they become programmable. All of the other principles follow from this first assertion.[17]

Modularity. New media texts are composed of discrete units and can be combined into larger objects without losing their independence. Some examples of this principle include the embedding of objects (images, charts, graphs) in word processing documents whose original sources may be independently edited, the distinct media elements in web pages, and the modular nature of the World Wide Web itself.

Automation. The first two principles, numerical representation (coding) and modular structure "allow for the automation of many operations involved in media creation, manipulation, and access" (32).

Variability. Also related to terms such as mutable and liquid, variability represents the non-fixed nature of new media. Variability is also a possible result of automation: "Instead of identical copies, a new media object typically gives rise to many different versions. And rather than being created completely by a human author, these versions are often in part automatically assembled by a computer" (36).

Transcoding. New media consist of two distinct layers—the cultural layer and the computer layer; "the logic of a computer can be expected to significantly influence the traditional cultural logic of media; that is, we may expect that the computer layer will affect the cultural layer" (46).

While Manovich provides a methodological approach, Packer and Jordan (2001) propose a different list of five elements. However, this list focuses on observable features of new media rather than principles. Packer and Jordan claim that these five characteristics of new media in aggregate define it as a medium distinct from all others:

Integration: the combining of artistic forms and technology into a hybrid form of expression.

Interactivity: the ability of the user to manipulate and affect her experience of media directly, and to communicate with others through media.

Hypermedia: the linking of separate media elements to one another that create a trail of personal association.

Immersion: the experience of entering into the simulation or suggestion of a three-dimensional environment.

Narrativity: aesthetic and formal strategies that derive from the above concepts, which result in nonlinear story forms and media presentation (xxxv).

One of the key differences in approach between Manovich's principles and Packer and Jordan's characteristics is that the latter can be more easily used when considering new media in terms of objects, while the former sees new media also in terms of processes of formation. Both of these lists, however, assume that new media is necessarily digital. Anne Wysocki (2004) proposes a very different approach, one that places the new media function in the hands of the designer:

We should call "new media texts" those that have been made by composers who are aware of the range of materialities of texts and who then highlight the materiality: such composers design texts that help readers/consumers/viewers stay alert to how any text—like its composers and readers—doesn't function independently of how it is made and in what contexts. (15)

One of the implications of this definition is that new media texts do not have to be digital. Wysocki uses Manovich's argument against using "interactivity" as a feature specific to new media because it is a contested term that may function both at the physical and psychological levels, and, as Wysocki notes, "his arguments portray how a process that can seem unique to digital texts can be more complexly connected to other ways we understand who we are and how we function" (2004, 17). Wysocki also works against Manovich's definition of new media as composed of computer data because "there are no human agents in that definition, with the implication that the process of translation [of existing media into numerical data] is natural and inexorable" (18).

Regardless of which definition of new media one uses, for digital rhetoric, it is an object of study that is subject to rhetorical theory and principles. Each of the proposed definitions and frameworks works well within a digital rhetoric context and each contributes to the theoretical and methodological approaches available to the digital rhetorician. A more explicit connection between new media and rhetoric is featured in Collin Brooke's (2009) *Lingua Fracta: Toward a Rhetoric of New Media*. The title of the work immediately situates new media as an object of study (as with "a rhetoric of technology" or "a rhetoric of science," each of which develops and catalogs the ways that specific uses of language and rhetorical practices embedded in those uses propel the persuasive power of technology and science, respectively). Brooke's project (to which I will refer in detail in chapter 2) "is located in between technology and rhetoric, using the canons [of classical rhetoric] to come to grips with new media at the same time that it acknowledges the changes that the canons must undergo in the context of new media" (xii). Brooke avoids the question of defining new media (although he references the contributions of both Manovich and Wysocki), and instead situates new media as a process or activity that occurs at the interface, which "functions as a dialectical space, in Burke's terms, and a rhetorical space *par excellence* . . . the interface is where rhetoric and technology meet" (xiii). Although he doesn't name it as such, Brooke's project is an excellent example of digital rhetoric scholarship that takes new media as its object of critique.

Human-Computer Interaction (HCI)

Having considered requirements, related rhetorical methods, and objects of study for digital rhetoric research and practice, I turn now to locating digital rhetoric as a field and its relationship to other, related fields, focusing on the examples of human-computer interaction (HCI) and the emergent field of critical code studies. I have chosen these two fields as examples because they come from very different disciplines and perspectives, yet both are closely related to digital rhetoric in terms of both methods and objects of study. One of the key connections between HCI and digital rhetoric is the importance of the interface—for digital rhetoric, the interface is both object and location; it serves as the point at which software, hardware, user, network, the virtual and the material come together. One of the key tasks for HCI is the development and programming of interfaces (which activity, I suggest, would benefit from collaboration with researchers who study the rhetorical functions of the interface).

HCI is an interdisciplinary field that draws on psychology, cognitive science, and sociology but is situated within computer science. In *Human-Computer Interaction*, Dix, Finlay, Abowd, and Beale (1993) claim that HCI "is, put simply, the study of people, computer technology, and the ways these influence each other" (xiii). Based on this very broad definition, it is clear that there are strong possible relationships between the work of HCI and digital rhetoric (indeed, that definition could just as well be a definition of digital rhetoric). However, much of the work of HCI is focused on producing hardware, software, and interfaces (rather than on communication, meaning-making, knowledge construction, or persuasion); in a way, HCI provides the tools and systems that support new media, networks, and other digital applications that digital rhetoric aims to study.

H. Rex Hartson (1998) offers a more specific definition:

> Human-Computer Interaction (HCI) is a field of research and development, methodology, theory, and practice, with the objective of designing, constructing, and evaluating computer-based interactive systems—including hardware, software, input/output devices, displays, training and documentation—so that people can use them efficiently, effectively, safely, and with satisfaction. (103)

While HCI is clearly more aligned with computer science and computer engineering than with communications, it shares with digital rhetoric (and a number of related writing-studies fields, such as technical communication and computers and writing) a focus on how people use technological systems to accomplish a wide range of tasks, and the deployment of terms such as "user" and "usability" also provide a connection between these fields. Thomas Skeen (2009), for instance, argues that "there is some overlap between the fields of rhetoric and HCI. One parallel is the issue of user empowerment. Whereas rhetoric . . . concerns itself with power, knowledge, and access by taking into consideration the different loci of power that exist simultaneously with users, designers, and the larger cultural context, the HCI field also concerns itself with user-centric empowerment as an ideal. As they consider the user's wants and needs, an ideal of democratization and empowerment exists in both fields" (102).

Given such an alignment of interests, it seems clear that a relationship between HCI and digital rhetoric would be mutually beneficial, particularly with regard to each field's interest in and commitment to usability. This is only one among several possible connections, but it is one whose interests are more obviously aligned with digital rhetoric than others. While HCI is one established field that could both benefit from and contribute to digital rhetoric, the same may hold true for emergent fields such as critical code studies and software studies.

Critical Code Studies

In 2006, Mark Marino proposed that the methods of literary analysis (in the form of critical hermeneutics) be applied to the reading of code. Marino situates his proposal as complementary to a number of new approaches that were developed around the same time, including software studies and platform studies. Unlike these other approaches, critical code studies is of interest because it relies explicitly on rhetorical methods. Each of these new fields is interested in a synthesis of humanities- and computer-science-based approaches to understanding how meaning is made at the human-computer interface; the primary difference is whether the focus should be on the platform (discrete systems that include both hardware and software, like the Nintendo Wii or Sony PlayStation), software, or code.

In the case of platform studies, researchers "[investigate] the relationships between the hardware and software design of computing systems and the creative works produced on those systems" (Bogost & Monfort 2006, n.p.). The Software Studies Initiative (2007), in contrast, takes a much wider view of the scope of software studies: "we think of software as a layer that permeates all areas of contemporary societies. Therefore, if we want to understand contemporary techniques of control, communication, representation, simulation, analysis, decision-making, memory, vision, writing, and interaction, our analysis can't be complete until we consider this software layer" (n.p). Critical code studies aims to examine the infrastructure behind the software by examining the code itself:

> Critical Code Studies (CCS) is an approach that applies critical hermeneutics to the interpretation of computer code, program architecture, and documentation within a socio-historical context. CCS holds that lines of code are not value-neutral and can be analyzed using the theoretical approaches applied to other semiotic systems in addition to particular interpretive methods developed particularly for the discussions of programs. (Marino 2006, n.p.)

Marino (2006) proposes that "we no longer speak of the code as a text in metaphorical terms, but that we begin to analyze and explicate code as a text, as a sign system with its own rhetoric, as verbal communication that possesses significance in excess of its functional utility. While computer scientists can theorize on the most useful approaches to code, humanities scholars can help by conjecturing on the meaning of code to all those who encounter it both directly by reading it or indirectly by encountering the effects of the programs it creates"—and it is this articulation of critical code studies that resonates as a digital rhetoric approach.

A 2011 HASTAC Scholars forum[18] suggested that critical code studies, as the practice of looking at code from a humanistic perspective, addresses questions such as

> What does it mean to look at the code not just from the perspective of what it "does" computationally, but how it works as a semiotic system, a cultural object, and as a medium for communication?
> How do issues of race, class, gender and sexuality emerge in the study of source code?

and

> What insights does code offer to the cultural critique of a digital object?

Much like literary studies is a branch of rhetoric that engages in a very focused examination of specific textual genres using a wide range of critical methods and theories, critical code studies can be seen as a subfield of digital rhetoric that takes code as its central object of study.

Digital Rhetoric, Digital Humanities, and Internet Studies

Critical code studies and human-computer interaction are only two examples among several possible where developing relationships with scholars and practitioners between these fields and digital rhetoric may be beneficial, and indeed this is certainly an incomplete map of the location of digital rhetoric with respect to other fields, disciplines, methods, and approaches. It is my hope that digital rhetoricians will continue to build networks and connections, extending the map (or even contesting my cartographic impulses by drawing new routes and new boundaries). Before continuing on to the chapters that review digital rhetoric theories, methods, and practices, I want to end this chapter with a consideration of two larger interdisciplinary constructions within which work on digital rhetoric circulates: digital humanities and Internet studies.

Digital humanities is currently used as a kind of catch-all description for a very broad range of approaches and methods that involve use of digital technologies (from geographical information systems, to 3-D modeling and simulation, to large-scale text mining and data visualization) to study humanities subjects (including history, art history, literature, and archaeology). Discussing the creation of the Office of Digital Humanities (ODH) within the National Endowment for the Humanities (NEH), director Brett Bobley (2008) explains that his office uses "'digital humanities' as an umbrella term for a number of different activities that surround technology and humanities scholarship. Under the digital humanities rubric, I would include topics like open access to materials, intellectual property rights, tool development, digital libraries, data mining, born-digital preservation, multimedia publication, visualization, GIS, digital reconstruction, study of the impact of technology on numerous fields, technology for teaching and learning, sustainability models, and many others" (1).

Despite this expansive view of topics, relatively few projects in digital rhetoric have been funded by the NEH; more projects have focused on developing tools and processes for working with historical works that have now been digitized. Bobley goes on to say that

> In one way or another, most of these digital humanities activities involve collections of cultural heritage materials, which are one of the primary objects of study for researchers across all humanities disciplines. Books, newspapers, journals, paintings, music, film, audio, sculpture, and other materials form a primary dataset for study. (1)

What's missing here is the development of collections of new cultural materials that are "born-digital" and the development of methods and methodologies for both studying and producing these new forms. I suspect that as the realm of digital humanities matures, there will be a strong turn in this direction, and I would suggest that digital rhetoric is well positioned to participate in and contribute to the digital humanities when it does so.

An additional concern comes from the position of rhetoric vis-à-vis the humanities more generally speaking. Historically, the core discipline of the humanities (from which others emerged over time) is rhetoric, yet rhetoric no longer appears to have a distinct identity as a discipline and is often overlooked as the foundation of the humanities. We can trace the problem back to Peter Ramus and his move to divorce all but style from the purview of rhetoric, as well as the way that nascent English departments drew on the works of Hugh Blair, Alexander Jamison, and other belletristic rhetoricians as the basis for the study of literature in the vernacular.[19] Digital rhetoric provides an opportunity to reclaim not just the neglected canons of memory and delivery, but to follow the work of contemporary rhetoricians who have been attempting to recover the full power of rhetoric and stake out a stronger claim within the continuing construction of digital humanities.

There are certainly ways that digital rhetoric can participate in the digital humanities alongside literary studies and history (particularly since the majority of methodologies in these disciplines are derived from rhetoric), but digital rhetoric also has much to offer the social science equivalent of the digital humanities, which is generally designated "Internet studies."

Internet studies emerged from the fields of computer-supported cooperative work (CSCW), sociology, and communications. Barry Wellman, one of the earliest advocates for applying a social network approach (see Wellman, 1997) to the Internet, traces the beginnings of the field to roughly 1994 and divides the first decade of its history into three "ages": theorizing the Internet (often uncritically); systematic documentation of users and uses; and real analysis based in theoretically driven projects (Wellman, 2004). To date, I have not seen digital rhetoric making many inroads in the conferences and journals of Internet studies. But there is a rich body of work that can contribute to digital rhetoric, particularly in terms of methods and methodologies (several of which will be discussed in chapter 3). At the same time, social networking theory is commensurate with a digital rhetoric approach to the study of networked communication, so there is also an opportunity to connect at the level of theory as well.

I end this chapter, then, with a charge to those of us who characterize our work as digital rhetoric—we must work to bring our theories and methods into the fields of the digital humanities and Internet studies because we have much to offer in both realms; we also have excellent opportunities to learn from and incorporate the work that is central to these fields as well.

TWO

Digital Rhetoric: Theory

When I began the project that eventually led to this book, I was interested in developing a theory of digital rhetoric, following Zappen (2005), who had suggested that scholars of rhetoric and technology should seek to craft a coherent digital rhetoric theory by synthesizing the various approaches that he cataloged in "Digital Rhetoric: Toward an Integrated Theory." However, there is such a wide range of digital domains and contexts that digital rhetoric may engage that I am instead convinced that, like visual rhetoric, digital rhetoric should be viewed as a field that engages multiple theories and methods rather than as a singular theory framework.

In the sections that follow, I will be reviewing current work on the development and extension of digital rhetoric theory. Generally, scholars have chosen to either apply the well-established theories of classical and contemporary rhetoric to digital texts and contexts or they have argued that the digital, networked, communication requires a revision or rearticulation of said theories. In other cases, the suggestion has been made that new forms of digital communication may require the development of a new rhetorical theory altogether, and several attempts have also been made to reframe theory from other disciplines and fields as inherently rhetorical (even if not explicitly understood as such except by rhetoricians). Because of the rapid pace of technological development and the relative youth of digital rhetoric as a field, I believe that there is value in each of these approaches, and I do not intend to privilege one over another; however, there are currently more examples of application and revision than there are of reframing and inventing new theories.

In terms of applying and revising traditional rhetorical theory, there is a distinct division between scholars who focus on classical rhetoric and those who prefer to engage contemporary theory. In this chapter, I will begin by reviewing approaches to classical rhetoric in terms of revising or reframing the five canons of rhetoric and then move to contemporary rhetorics by looking at the rhetorical situation, identity, networks, and digital ecologies, economies, and circulation. I have provided an overview of selected works in each of these areas in order to show a range of approaches and applications, but these references are certainly not exhaustive. As with digital rhetoric methods and practices, it is possible to claim that nearly all work that addresses digital communication can be considered part of digital rhetoric; however, I have endeavored to principally focus on work that explicitly situates itself within digital rhetoric and closely related fields.

Digitizing Classical Rhetoric

Most treatments of digital rhetoric focus on more contemporary work of theorists like Roland Barthes, Mikhail Bakhtin, Kenneth Burke, and Michel Foucault, among others; until recently, connections between classical rhetoric and digital media have typically not moved beyond applying traditional rhetorical analysis of the role of ethos, pathos, and logos in online texts. James Zappen's (2005) "Digital Rhetoric: Toward an Integrated Theory" addresses the use of these three primary rhetorical appeals but focuses primarily on issues of identity and community as engaged by current rhetorical theory. The first work to fully engage classical rhetoric as a foundation for digital rhetoric theory is Kathleen Welch's (1999) *Electric Rhetoric: Classical Rhetoric, Oralism, and a New Literacy*. Welch uses Isocrates as a key figure of classical rhetoric, arguing for the "redeployment of Sophistic classical rhetoric" as a key move in developing a rhetorical theory that can account for the persuasive affordances of electronic media. Welch draws on the recovery work performed in the 1980s and 1990s by Cheryl Glenn, C. Jan Swearingen, Susan Jarrett, Richard Enos, Edward Schiappa, Takis Poulakos, and Victor Vitanza, then adds to this work her own construction of Isocrates as Sophist: in her argument, "classical Greek rhetoric and writing practices are Isocratic, which is to say Sophistic, intersubjective, performative, and a merger of oralism and literacy" (12). More recently, Collin Brooke (2009) undertakes a complete reconfiguration of the classical canons of rhetoric in *Lingua Fracta: Towards a Rhetoric of New Media*. While others have focused on a specific canon (such as memory or delivery) and their application or rearticulation in the face of digital texts, thus far only Brooke has provided a comprehensive consideration of all of the canons, describing their complex inter-relationships as an ecology of practice: "As an ecology of practice, the canons supply a framework for approaching new media that focuses on the strategies and practices that occur at the level of interface" (28).

Recovering the Sophists for a Digital Age

Sophistic rhetoric, with its focus on both literacy and orality and a clear sense of situated activity and sociocultural relativism, certainly is well suited for addressing issues of multimedia presentation and the function of digital text circulation within particular social and electronic networks. In part, sophistic rhetoric is useful for exactly the reasons that got it into trouble with Plato: in her discussion of the *Pre-Socratic Philosophers*, Kathleen Freeman (1966) indicates that Plato felt that the sophistic principles of cultural relativism disavowed "any possibility of stable knowledge of any kind" (349), thus suggesting also that "objects do not exist except while someone is perceiving them" (349). Indeed, digital objects do not exist in the material sense apart from observation, activity, and use (either by humans or by technological actors). Another feature of sophistic rhetoric that argues for its importance to digital rhetoric is its focus on probability (and denial of absolute truth): "Acknowledging an epistemological status for probability demands in discourse a flexible process of ordering or arranging, a feature of both *nomos* (a social construct involving ordering) and narrative" (Jarratt, 1991, 47).

While relatively few scholars have focused on the Sophists (in part because we have less original material to work with), Welch's (1999) *Electric Rhetoric* provides an exemplary study in the use of sophistic rhetoric as applied to digital contexts.

Blakesley and Brooke (2001) and LaGrandeur (2003), among others, have singled out the work of Gorgias as prefiguring the value of visual rhetoric within the digital context, and Scott Reed (2009) characterizes "the rhetorical scene of 4th and 5th Century BCE Greece as something of a cybernetic system, one in which the conversation/conflict between Plato and the Sophists (particularly Gorgias, in my limited reading) can be viewed as a meeting ground between distinct approaches to medial 'extension'" (51).

In an earlier call to revive and use sophistic rhetoric, Michelle Ballif (1998) links the figure of the cyborg with the Sophist to create a "Third Sophistic Cyborg" that functions "not as a rhetorical subject/political agent in any traditional sense, but rather as a rhetorical figure that embodies postmodern rhetorical practices" (53). Her aim is to show how this form of rhetoric might radicalize politics and democracy; it is a large-scale project that envisions a new kind of rhetor for a digital age: "The Third Sophist . . . is suggesting a rhetorical situation negotiated by *metis* rather than mastered by *techne*; and the cunning Cyborg is the figure (which is not One, but a network) that navigates the postmodern discursive world . . ." (67).

Recovering the Sophists for digital rhetoric can take place at the level of the image, the action, the process, or on the much grander scale of reforming rhetoric itself. It strikes me that there is still much productive work that could be done in digital rhetoric with regard to understanding and applying sophistic rhetorics to digital contexts, and I hope that we will see an increased focus not just on the relationship of Aristotelian-and-after classical rhetoric but a continuation of this kind of recovery work.

The Canons of Classical Rhetoric

I address the main elements of the rhetorical canon—invention, arrangement, style, delivery, and memory—in terms of their relation to the production of digital texts; I aim to focus, as the Roman rhetoricians did, more on production than on analysis, as Lauer (2004) indicates when she notes that "interpreters of . . . Roman rhetoricians, discussing their epistemologies, have often described their concept of rhetorical invention as a practical art concerned with the 'how,' not the 'why'" (23).

It may appear at first glance that I will be leaning rather heavily on Aristotelian constructions because I am using his canon of rhetorical practices as an organizing principle (which should be no surprise; Aristotle is nothing if not an expert taxonomist—perhaps the finest information architect of his day). But, as Porter and Sullivan (1994) aptly note, "[b]ecause rhetoric is a situated and applied art, it generates *principles*, not *rules*. The difference is significant: principles are always interpreted and adjusted for situations (and rarely survive in pure form); rules circumscribe absolute boundaries" (115); in using Aristotle's framework, I hope to provide an anchor for the generation of principles—at the same time, I hope to avoid his tendency toward declamation of specific rules and dicta. In some respects, Aristotle's rhetorical canon may not be ideal for a taxonomy of digital practices because there is a great deal of overlap between invention and arrangement and even of invention and style when considering the production of digital compositions; thus the divisions are, like the digital works they aim to describe, porous.

Brooke (2009) argues that the "canons can help us understand new media, which add to our understanding of the canons as they have evolved with contemporary technologies. Neither rhetoric nor technology is left unchanged in their encounter" (201)—so there is a reciprocity at work as we consider the canons in light of digital rhetoric practices and new media objects. One approach that we can take is a fairly simple mapping of digital practices to classical uses of the canon, as presented in the table below:

But this kind of mapping doesn't surface the kind of reciprocal interaction that Brooke describes, instead keeping the canons intact as reified monuments rather than the flexible schema we need for them to continue to work after their encounter with digital texts. In each of the next sections, I'll take a look at the canons individually and note scholars (like Brooke) who have worked to reimagine or reframe the canons for use within a digital rhetoric.

Invention

In Aristotle's famous formulation, rhetoric is "the art (*techne*) of finding out the available means of persuasion" (1991, 37), and the primary means of finding these means is through the faculty of invention, which describes "how individuals might employ a theoretical framework to discover arguments that might be effective in public deliberation and judgment" (Sauer, 2003, 3). Michael Leff (1983) similarly describes Cicero's inventional topics of person and act as a shift from the Aristotelian "discovery of inferential connectives to the discovery of the materials for arguments" (29); according to Leff, Cicero's system (as described in *De Oratore*) also rejects Aristotle's strict division of dialectical and rhetorical theories of invention, drawing on both to provide an emphasis on discovery that privileged the establishment of logical relationships and the creation of categories of topics based on the subject of the discourse (30–31). Cicero's model of invention, then, can be described in terms of links (relationships) and lexia (materials). Renato Barilli (1989) also argues that Cicero overturned Aristotle's model of dialectic over rhetoric because Cicero valued the forum over the chamber, maintaining that Cicero refused to privilege content and meaning over modes, signifiers, situations, or contexts and that the probable for Cicero has a historical and temporal dimension (27–

TABLE 2.1

Canon	Classical Definition/Use	Digital Practice
Invention	finding available means of persuasion	searching and negotiating networks of information; using multimodal and multimedia tools
Arrangement	formalized organization	manipulating digital media as well as selecting ready-made works and reconstituting them into new works; remixing
Style	ornamentation/appropriate form	understanding elements of design (color, motion, interactivity, font choice, appropriate use of multimedia, etc.)
Delivery	oral presentation	understanding and using systems of distribution (including the technical frameworks that support varying protocols and networks)
Memory	memorization of speech	information literacy—knowing how to store, retrieve, and manipulate information (personal or project-based; blogs or databases)

28). Thus, Cicero's model is also particularly appropriate for understanding networked rhetoric, which is metaphorically more forum than chamber, and which creates meaning through shared historical, temporal, and geographical contexts.

Casting invention as a process of discovery fits current practices of digital production in two respects: in the most common case, writers seek out materials to inspire—and in some cases to incorporate into—their own digital work; but rhetors also use the capacity of invention-as-discovery to invent new digital forms as well. Invention, as a function of digital rhetoric, includes the searching and negotiation of networks of information, seeking those materials best suited to creating persuasive works, as well as knowing which semiotic resources to address and draw upon (aural, visual, textual, hypertextual) and what technological tools are best suited to working with those resources.

Invention also takes place through interactions with other texts (including engagement with multimodal/multimedia digital objects and electronic discourse with other people). As Collin Brooke (2009) notes, new media texts foreground both "a more social model of invention" and "a model that is concerned more with practice than product" (82). For example, in a case of blogging by citizen-journalists, Damien Pfister (2011) argues that a "fundamental contribution that bloggers make to public deliberation" is "the invention of novel arguments. It is not just that bloggers simply pay attention to certain issues, thus directing the focus of the press; it is their ability to (occasionally) invent arguments worth taking up in broader spheres of public engagement" (152). This process of invention happened through social interaction rather than as an individual process of discovery (which is the more common approach to understanding invention in terms of writing pedagogies in composition/rhetoric). Ryan Skinnell (2010) makes a similar point in an investigation of responses to a widely circulated video on YouTube. Skinnell also situates YouTube as an archive, arguing that the archive (as cultural practice of memory) can serve as a site of invention:

> archives are incomplete traces of past events. . . . [I]n Derrida's theory of archives, however, this incompleteness is not a barrier, but an imperative of archives that invites users to invent the narratives that make the traces seem whole. . . . The archives may determine what can be wrought from them, but the fundamental incompleteness of materials leaves spaces for users to invent connections that make the archives salient and comprehensible. (n.p.)

These gaps in the archive are a less extreme form of Hilst's (2011) directive to experiment with nonbeing as a mode of invention as it invites users to examine the elements of the archive that are not-there and respond to said archival incompleteness.

Rhetorical invention in networked digital contexts arises from user interaction both with archives and with other users, but it also is enacted and used individually but any given writer. Elizabeth Tomlinson (2011) suggests that "digitized rhetorical invention encompasses aspects of both idea creation and discovery, particularly as manifested through writers' audience considerations and their descriptions of their writing processes. By further deconstructing the artificial binary, digital invention can be more effectively and usefully interpreted according to a socio-cognitive framework . . . which acknowledges spaces for both social influences and individual subjectivities" (63). The interaction of the social and individual, and the resistance of closure (in a sense, the experimentation with nonbeing), undergirds Brooke's reframing of invention as proairesis (action) as opposed to hermeneusis (interpretation). Brooke contends that "hermeneutic invention relies on the relative sturdiness of a final object and the negotiation of meanings within it . . . much of our theorizing about invention in rhetoric and composition remains bound by the particular media for which we invent" (68). For new media texts, there may be no "final object" as such (and if there is one, it may well resist "sturdiness" altogether); thus an understanding of invention for digital rhetoric should resist closure. Brooke uses social bookmarking services (sites like del.icio.us and citeulike) as an example of a digital invention practice that both engages social interaction and resists closure or completion in a way that privileges invention-as-action over invention-as-interpretation.

Brooke's take on invention follows in part from the distinction that Gregory Ulmer (2003) has made between heuristics and what he calls "heuretics"—"the use of theory to invent forms and practices, as distinct from 'hermeneutics,' which uses theory to interpret existing works" (4). In *Internet Invention*, Ulmer provides a kind of textbook-in-progress designed to introduce a new framework of invention for digitally mediated texts and images that are read not through traditional forms of literacy but through "electracy" ("a neologism coined to distinguish the emerging apparatus from the established one" [28]). Ulmer suggests that orality and literacy served specific socio-cultural institutions and that with each change in dominant medium, new institutions will arise: "In the same way that Socrates, Plato, and Aristotle did not ask how writing might serve the needs of the institutions of orality—religion, ritual, magic—but instead invented a new institution—school—and new practices native to writing (method, dialogue), it is my responsibility . . . to find an equivalent for electracy" (28–29). This equivalent institution he calls the "EmerAgency," which is a kind of collaborative consulting practice for digitally produced investigations. Ulmer explicitly states that "the EmerAgency is a practice for invention" and opines that he is "optimistic about the possibility of the EmerAgency to facilitate the formation of digital rhetoric, even if it is not the rhetoric that I propose, since it does not claim absolutely to be that rhetoric, but rather a means to invent an appropriate internet practice" (28).

Invention, then, is not just the collection of resources that can be deployed in the development of an argument, and it is also more than the new arguments found through interaction with new media texts and through online social discourse—invention in digital rhetoric leads to new kinds of text, new forms of meaning, new practices of production, and potentially new institutions. Invention is also tied explicitly to arrangement, which can also facilitate invention in its application.

Arrangement

Arrangement in classical rhetoric is typically a formal system of organization that delineates each part of a speech based on its purpose: Aristotle (who was more concerned with invention than arrangement) recommended four parts, Cicero suggested six divisions, and Quintilian divided the oration into five parts (the genesis of the five-paragraph essay). For classical rhetoricians, though, this system of organization was not fixed and orators where not bound to follow the conventions in every case. Doug Brent (1997) suggests that in classical rhetoric, "arrangement is determined more by the context, the audience, the rhetorical purpose—the cluster of exigencies that rhetoricians refer to as *kairos*—than by a 'logical' progression of propositions" (n.p.).

While arrangement for digital works is still intimately tied to *kairos*, it shifts radically away even from the organic principles of organization suggested by classical rhetoric when new media works can be constructed nonlinearly. However, there is one hallmark of classical arrangement that is actually better suited to digital composition than to print composition. As Jane Walpole (1981) contends, "unlike its modern namesake, the classical concept of arrangement focused on the seven parts of an oration: introduction, narration, exposition, proposition, confirmation, confutation, and conclusion. This sequence is clearly designed to help a listening audience follow an oral argument. It teems with repetitions, restatements, familiar examples, expected patterns—clear characteristics of oral literacy" (66). While Walpole argues that these cues are unnecessary for readers (e.g., because they can refer back to previous pages of text), they take on new importance in digital rhetoric, where the thread of organization may not be the same for all audiences.

In digital rhetoric, arrangement may be a conscious decision of the writer of the digital text, but it may also be left up to the user, as in the case of hypertext, where the reader creates a new arrangement with each reading. In this case, arrangement is more of a boundary condition, *as the possible arrangements are limited by the number of nodes and the links between* them that have been established by the author. In this case, arrangement functions architecturally, and Brooke draws on Quintilian's architectural metaphor (from Book VII of *Institutio Oratoria*) to explain that "just because there is more than one way to walk through a building, this does not make its arrangement (architecture) irrelevant. So too with hypertexts" whose "links . . . are rhetorical practices of arrangement, attempts to communicate affinities, connections, and relationships" (91).

Arrangement can also be seen as an emergent feature of digital texts, as an element that is contingent rather than fixed. Brooke (2009) has further suggested that we reframe the traditional canon of arrangement as "pattern"— and in so doing, we open up a range of opportunities for both analysis and production. Brooke notes that the database, seen as a cultural form (per Manovich, 2001, 219), becomes a rhetorical text: "Although databases may contain no predetermined order, they are useful to us to the degree that they provide some sort of order when they are acted on by users" (101)—and the patterns that emerge from such database use, from the "related purchases" system of Amazon to those provided from the output of search engine use, constitute a new formulation of arrangement for digital rhetoric. At the level of method, "the construction of small-scale databases can create the conditions of possibility for the kind of pattern and relationship analysis carried out under the umbrella of data mining" (107).

A more active form of emergent arrangement occurs through the process of "tagging"—individual users add descriptive tags to links, sites, or media objects that can form an arrangement when many users' tags are aggregated (this arrangement comes about organically and is referred to as a "folksonomy"). Jeff Rice (2010), for instance, speaks of "tagging" as a new system of arrangement as "the student, the text, the word, the image, and so on are tagged in relationships" and the rhetorical process of arrangement is invoked through the importance of "getting . . . ideas labeled in a variety of ways and delivered to an audience" (64). In this case, the folksonomy of tagging leads to an emergent arrangement, but the digital rhetorician can engage strategies that will help shape how it does so.

Digital rhetoric in many ways erodes the distance between rhetor and reader, producer and user. In terms of arrangement, we can consider interface customization as mechanism for allowing the user to decide upon an ideal individual arrangement—as for instance, Photoshop's floating tool palette allows the user to rearrange the elements of the interface upon the surface of the screen. As in the discussion of hypertext, this represents the architectural sense of arrangement and demonstrates that it is available as a rhetorical function for both users and makers of digital texts.

For digital rhetoric, arrangement is also a productive art—not just a method for carrying forth a logical, cohesive argument. A theory of digital arrangement must include the practices of manipulating digital media as well as selecting ready-made works and reconstituting them into new works. As Lawrence Lessig (2005) points out, culture is made through the process of remixing, which is a confluence of invention and arrangement. Both Warnick (2007) and Hilst (2011) note the importance of juxtaposition as a form of arrangement that serves as a key rhetorical method for remix production. Thus, unlike Aristotle's formulation, where arrangement appears less important than invention, for a theory of digital rhetoric, the two are intimately tied together. Just as important for digital text production is the canon of style.

Style

Aristotle notes that "the whole business of rhetoric [is] concerned with appearance" (165), and thus style is an important consideration. For Aristotle, style was primarily a question of matching the appropriate forms of language to the discourse at hand, but he also had several suggestions for developing effective style (including an emphasis on correctness, use of appropriate metaphor, and an avoidance of excessively ornamental prose). Style is an important element of rhetoric but not, as Peter Ramus would have it, the only element of rhetoric. As Gideon Burton (2004) notes, "from a rhetorical perspective style is not incidental, superficial, or supplementary: style names how ideas are embodied in language and customized to communicative contexts . . . ornamentation was not at all superficial in classical and renaissance rhetoric, for to ornament (*ornare* = "to equip, fit out, or supply") meant to equip one's thoughts with verbal expression appropriate for accomplishing one's intentions" (n.p.).

Style takes on new importance for digital rhetoric, particularly in terms of visual style: for a digital rhetoric, style is equivalent to "design"; thus, digital rhetoric must be concerned with understanding all the available elements of document design, including color, font choice, and layout, as well as multimedia design possibilities such as motion, interactivity, and appropriate use of media. Style in this sense is also an important quality in terms of a given text's use and usability. Bradley Dilger (2010) reminds us that for rhetoric, "style is never optional, as the common sense opposition of style to substance wrongly indicates" (16); rather, it is an integral element of all rhetorical communication and the question is not whether we want style or substance, but what kind of style we want to deploy as a component of substance. Brendan Riley (2010), noting that "Web writers have begun styling their work," argues that "if acquiring the ability to control one's speech gives one power, so must the ability to control one's style" and goes as far as declaring that "digital writing is style" (77).

Lanham (2006) argues that in an information economy, "attention is the commodity in short supply" (xi) and it is attention that is needed to make sense of the overwhelming availability of information in its raw state. And "the devices that regulate attention are stylistic devices. Attracting attention is what style is all about." Lanham suggests that we need to develop a faculty that helps us understand the relationship of style and substance in digital texts, a "bi-stable way of examining an expressive surface, through for meaning, and at for style" (256). Following Lanham, an example of style's function with regard to attention is Teena Carnegie's (2009) work on the interface as *exordium* (an attention-getting device) through its fundamental features of multi-directionality, manipulability, and presence.

Not everyone fully agrees with Lanham's project—Dilger (2010), for instance, argues that "his approach maintains the style and substance dichotomy. For me, it would be better to shift the definition of style . . . to more fully acknowledge its connection to and inclusion of substance—the commonalities of stylistic elements of all kinds, not only those manifested in surface features" (16).[1] For both Lanham and Dilger, though, style has shifted from a limiting and limited approach to the purpose and function of rhetoric and regained access to its full faculties within the rhetorical canon as it is applied to digital texts. If style has always been a part of rhetoric, memory has been at times neglected, but is making a comeback with the advent of digital rhetoric.

Memory

Memory in the classical rhetoric canon was concerned with memorization of speeches but also with the function of memory in developing a store of rhetorical arguments and practices that the rhetoric could draw upon at will; indeed, the *Rhetorica ad Herennium* describes memory as "treasury of things invented." With the advent of alphabetic literacy, memory became less of a central concern of rhetoric—writing itself took up the processes that previously were delegated to the memory of the individual orator. In this way, memory began to serve a broader population, as social and cultural memories could be inscribed and archived (as, for instance, in libraries). Foucault's notion of the archive is also useful here, not just as a form of memory but as a system that interacts with the statement: statements are a dynamic part of communication and will change the archive—both physically, with new requests changing the substance of the rhetorical objects in the archive, but also by changing the conceptual frames through which we can interpret the archive (Foucault, 1972, 135).

A number of scholars in composition/rhetoric and technical communication have begun the work of recovering memory—a canon that had been all but abandoned in the application of rhetoric to print texts in the teaching of composition. John Walter (2005), for instance, has suggested that metadata tagging of digital texts functions as digital mnemonics or ways of remembering significant information about digital documents. Similarly, Porter (2005) argues that rhetoricians should be concerned with recovering memory as a method for both the recovery of artifacts ("missing and lost works, traditions, arts; culture and language . . . 're-memory' on an individual as well as a cultural level" [n.p.]) and the preservation of artifacts (archiving, storage, and tracking of digital material). This last point is particularly important given both the ephemeral nature of digital texts as they circulate within unstable networks and the malleability of digital work (there is no guarantee of an "authoritative" work if all digital work can be easily manipulated and remixed). In a study of medieval illuminated manuscripts, Kathie Gossett (2008) argues that memory served as praxis in medieval rhetoric and that it has a potentially valuable role to play in composition pedagogy that focuses on multimodal and new media production; other scholars have turned to the canon of memory to inform the development of digital systems, such as Stewart Whittemore's (2008) application of memoria to the development of content management systems.

Brooke (2009) argues that a view of memory reduced to "a question of storage, as if memory simply signified the retention or location of quantifiable amounts of information" (143–44), closes off more rhetorical approaches to the use of memory in new media texts. He notes that "although memory is a canon that focuses our attention on the relationship between discourse and time, the treatment of memory as storage spatializes the canon, reducing it to the single axis of presence and absence" (148). He suggests that digital rhetoric requires a shift from memory-as-storage only to seeing memory as a range of practices, one of which is memory-as-persistence. Brooke calls this form of memory "persistence of cognition" and defines persistence as a memory practice as "the ability to build and maintain patterns, although those patterns may be tentative and ultimately fade into the background . . . persistence is a practice of bricolage" (157); in other words, memory is once again an activity (as it was originally situated in the classical sense), not just a repository.

While the work of Brooke, Gossett, Whittemore, and others represent the beginning of a renewed interest in the canon of memory, there has been an even stronger surge in work that aims to recover the other "lost" canon—delivery.

Delivery

Delivery, like style and memory, takes on a new importance when considered as an element of digital composition. Digital rhetoric needs to provide methods for understanding and using systems of distribution and publication (including the technical frameworks that support varying protocols and networks), but this must be coupled with a broader theory of circulation. James Porter (2005) has also delineated several important facets of digital delivery, including access, interaction, and economics; he argues that a theory of digital delivery must include both productive practices and a method of developing ethical *phronêsis*. (See also DeVoss and Porter [2006] for an extended discussion of delivery and ethics and Porter [2009] for an expanded view of digital delivery that consists of five key topics—Body/Identity, Distribution/Circulation, Access/Accessibility, Interaction, and Economics.) Digital delivery also needs to take into account the performative aspects of digital composition (particularly with regard to multimedia work). However, Porter notes that the individual elements of his theory "don't have very much generative or productive power unless you put them into dynamic interaction with each other and with other rhetorical topics. In other words, you connect up questions of delivery with rhetorical invention, with audience, with design of a web site, and so on" (Porter, 2005, n.p.).

A number of scholars have seen delivery in networked systems as circulation of digital texts, following John Trimbur's (2000) argument that circulation should be re-introduced in writing instruction; however, his definition of circulation is as an element or result of delivery. Trimbur suggests that

> neglecting delivery has led writing teachers to equate the activity of composing with writing itself and to miss altogether the complex delivery systems through which writing circulates. By privileging composing as the main site of instruction, the teaching of writing has taken up what Karl Marx calls a "one-sided" view of production and thereby has largely erased the cycle that links the production, distribution, exchange, and consumption of writing. This cycle of interlocked moments is what Marx calls *circulation*. (190)

My view of circulation as distinct from but effected by delivery is at odds with Trimbur's conflation of Marx's concept of circulation and the rhetorical practice of delivery. This is partly due to complications that arise from addressing the issue of consumption of social capital and partly due to Marx's use of circulation to refer to the entire process of production, distribution, exchange, and consumption; I see circulation as influential in each of these activities, but not as a container for them.

A great deal of work on delivery has been undertaken, both in composition/rhetoric (such as Yancey's [2006] collection, *Delivering College Composition: The Fifth Canon*) and in digital rhetoric. James Ridolfo (2005), for instance, has developed techniques that aid the writer in developing what he calls "rhetorical velocity," tying into the notion of delivery as not just a transaction but as successful communication (or, as Lanham puts it in his discussion of delivery, "communicating the message in such a way that it would be accepted and attended to rather than refused, ignored, or thrown in the wastepaper basket unread" [24]). Ridolfo and DeVoss (2009) provide additional application of these techniques in "Composing for Recomposition: Rhetorical Velocity and Delivery."

Brooke (2009) argues that we need to see delivery not only as transitive or transactional but also as "intransitive, constitutive *performance*" (170, emphasis in original), suggesting that "it is debatable whether new media exists outside of performance . . . a discussion list is simply a list of email addresses, for example; it is only in the performance, the consensual invocation of a discussion space that the list exists as a medium for conversation" (181)—and if that is the case, delivery (as performance) is absolutely integral to digital rhetoric.

Digital Rhetoric and Contemporary Rhetorical Theory

The literature that draws on contemporary rhetorical theory—from Foucault, to Derrida, to Covino, to Deleuze and Guattari—to inform digital texts, new media, systems, networks, and digitally mediated organizations is vast. Indeed, many of the scholars who work on reframing or reimagining the classical canon of rhetoric draw on contemporary theorists to make their arguments, so, in a sense, we have already covered the influence of contemporary theory on digital rhetoric. Rather than collating a massive number of citations or presenting an annotated bibliography that would be longer than this book all by itself, I instead focus on three areas of contemporary theory that have seen recent interest in the field. These three areas focus on reframing the notion of the rhetorical situation, the relationship between digital rhetoric and the formation of digital identities, and the appropriation and use of network by digital rhetoric scholars.

The Rhetorical Situation

The notion of the rhetorical situation serves as lens that frames a particular rhetorical activity within a set frame, thus allowing analysis to take place within a context that is created through the interaction of rhetoric, text, audience, and rhetorical purpose. Since its introduction by Lloyd Bitzer (1968), the concept of the rhetorical situation has been challenged, mediated, and reframed; the digital texts and networked spaces of digital rhetoric have prompted a renewed interest in the rhetorical situation and whether it can be applied to digital contexts as well as more traditional rhetorical activity.

Bitzer begins by theorizing rhetoric as a response to a specific need or exigence, which is a problem that requires a response: "an imperfection marked by urgency; it is a defect, an obstacle, something waiting to be done, a thing which is other than it should be" (6). It also must be a problem that can be addressed through discourse; this exigence is a necessary condition of rhetoric, and it calls rhetoric into existence as a response. Bitzer's construction of the rhetorical situation includes three key elements: exigence, audience, and constraints. Exigence produces the situation, which "controls the rhetorical response. . . . Not the rhetor and not persuasive intent, but the situation is the source and ground of rhetorical activity" (6). The audience, in Bitzer's framework, must be "capable of being influenced by discourse and of being mediators of change" (8); constraints are "made up of persons, events, objects, and relations which are parts of the situation because they have the power to constrain decision and action needed to modify the exigence" (8).

In response to Bitzer's construction, Richard Vatz (1973) argued that situation does not exist separately from rhetoric, nor does it call it into being by virtue of exigence; rather, rhetors establish situations through the choice to engage in rhetorical discourse. The rhetorical situation, in Vatz's view, is a product of perception rather than an independent, objective phenomenon. Steve Krause (1996) notes that Vatz's is "a position which is reminiscent of Gorgias': since 'nothing' (in the sense of ideal essences) exists, and since humans are inherently limited by perceptions, rhetors use language to *create* situations" (n.p., emphasis in original).

The following year, Scott Consigny (1974) suggested that the views of Bitzer and Vatz were two parts of a more complex approach to rhetorical situation. Consigny suggests that through *techne*, rhetors can "discover the real issues in indeterminate situations," manage "real situations and bringing them to a successful resolution or closure," and "can function in all kinds of indeterminate and particular situations as they arise" (180)—rhetorical invention thus may function as discovery and creation, depending on the need of the rhetor. Consigny does mediate Vatz's position as well, noting that rhetors do not exist outside of their own contexts and cannot by themselves bring a rhetorical situation into being.

While a number of theorists have continued to focus on rhetorical situation (such as Miller [1984], and Biesecker [1999], among others), the concept has more recently been called into question in terms of its ability to address digital texts and contexts. The following three examples represent approaches that broaden the scope of the rhetorical situation in response to digital rheto-ric: Steve Krause (1996) develops a theory of immediacy to articulate the idea of the Internet "as both an example and a generator of immediate rhetorical situations"; Jenny Edbauer (2005) argues for a shift from rhetorical situation to rhetorical ecology; and Fatima Pashaei (2010) applies Edbauer's approach in order to develop an ecology of blogging that follows Krause's collapse of the distinction between rhetor and audience in digital discourse.

Krause's (1996) work reimagines the rhetorical situation through the lens of postmodern critical theory, grounding his approach through a method of what he terms "immediacy":

> Immediacy and immediate rhetorical situations question the distinctions between audiences and rhetors, highlight the multiplicity of avenues of discourse within any given situation, and attempt to account for a dis-course that seemingly takes place *outside* any physical situation and be-tween fragmented/ contradictory/ multiplicitous selves. . . . [I]mmediacy is a much more fluid and dynamic reading of rhetorical situations that at-tempts to examine how discourse functions (or doesn't function) within a postmodernist, technologically-advanced mode where the static distinc-tions assumed by "modernist" rhetoricians like Plato, Gorgias, Bitzer, and Vatz are no longer valid. (n.p.)

The first principle of immediacy is the collapse of many of the distinctions that provide the framework for more traditional versions of the rhetorical situation, such as cause, effect, rhetor, audience, and message—"immediate rhetorical situations are first and foremost those which cannot trace their ori-gins (or, in Bitzer's terms, 'exigence') to any singular cause" (n.p.). Krause uses examples from discussion lists and Usenet, showing the difficulty of tracing the thread of a discussion to its origins; I would suggest that this ef-fect is even more apparent in Twitter, which functions more as a continuous stream than a discrete conversation. Additionally, with the instability of the web itself, with sites constantly vanishing and moving, the lack of a discover-able origin point highlights the way that "postmodern situations also prob-lematize and fragment unifying concepts of time, place, and identity" (n.p.). Refiguring the rhetorical situation through postmodern theory ultimately provides more questions than answers, but they are productive questions that have been taken up over the past decade and that continue to shape digital rhetoric theory.

An approach that implicitly follows Krause's construction is the move to see the rhetorical situation in ecological terms, thus allowing a given situation to exist within complex networks of interaction that are more fluid than traditional media would allow. Jenny Edbauer (2005) argues that "rhetorical situations operate within a network of lived practical consciousness or structures of feeling," and, like Krause, she suggests that "placing the rhetorical 'elements' within this wider context destabilizes the discrete borders of a rhetorical situation" (5). Edbauer proposes "a revised strategy for theorizing public rhetorics (and rhetoric's publicness) as a circulating ecology of effects, enactments, and events," simultaneously adding "the dimensions of history and movement (back) into our visions/versions of rhetoric's public situations" (9). While not specifically applying the frame of rhetorical ecologies to digital contexts, Edbauer's call to see the rhetorical situation in ecological terms fits very well with digital rhetoric approaches, and in the final example in this section, Fatima Pashaei uses Edbauer's ecological framework to situate a study of blogs.

Pashaei (2010) examines blogs about Muslim identity and practices and uses her analysis to complicate notions of exigence and audience as elements of the rhetorical situation and to support her claim that "the co-creation of rhetoric (by writers and their publics) in the blogosphere is transforming not only how discourse is generated and circulated in the public, but also the blog genre itself" (39). Following Edbauer, she rejects the view of the rhetorical situation as a series of fixed elements and instead argues that an ecological approach can better "account for the multitude of possibilities for interaction and engagement between writers and their discursive publics, as discourse circulates through various environments, spaces, times, and societies" (65). In order to better represent the element of movement that a rhetorical ecology model foregrounds, Pashaei redesigns the classic rhetorical triangle as an atom, with all of the elements in motion. The model she builds is specific to the genre she is analyzing, but it has promise as a model for digital rhetoric.

Pashaei's model highlights the dynamic nature of rhetorical practice and "accounts for multiple exigencies that drive interactions between the author (blogger) and the public (discursive) as the blog's rhetoric circulates in time, space and society" (33).

Pashaei's case-study approach not only examines blogging in terms of rhetorical ecologies and circulation but also examines how the genre of the blog represents public constructions of Muslim identity—and it is the question of identity as a rhetorical construct (both online and off) that I turn to next.

Digital Rhetoric and Digital Identity

Identity has been a concern for digital rhetoric since the advent of networking technologies, and quite a few scholars have theorized how digital space complicates, facilitates, or subverts the very notion of individual identity. Early works tended toward a quasi-utopian view that the digital self, represented through conscious choices in and across networks, would leave behind the body, with its attendant baggage of race, class, and gender. More recent work calls into question the warrant of that claim, since the body—especially in digital form—is a discursive formation that resists the dissociation of the physical and the virtual, and still others are now turning to the antiutopian view that technology may be damaging in its utilization of power outside of the physical body. Jimmie Killingsworth (2010), for example, argues "for the cyberhuman of the postmodern world, the body is not the core of identity so much as an element in a distributed identity that includes machines as well as other people. The problem of thus identifying the body with machines is that we may come to think of the body—and, by extension, other people—as something we use. Becoming users of the body rather than a body itself, we are prone to *overuse* or even *abuse* the body" (83, emphasis in original). The notion of "distributed identity" can be seen as either positive or negative, and the value of technology to make and sustain social ties over geographic distances has contributed to the construction of such distributed identities as they are tied to social and cultural organizations:

> As a result of the weakening of traditional ties in late modernity, people look towards virtual communities as social loci for the re-negotiation and construction of their identities. The ambiguous and complex environment of cyberspace becomes a new arena for the articulation of the politics of recognition, generating hybrid collective formations, such as digital nations, virtual diasporas and other online communities of an ethnic/national orientation. (Diamandaki, 2003, n.p.)

In treatments of classical rhetoric, identity has often been tied to ethos, but ethos has also been reframed as an appeal that may be absent an identity (and the representation of character and decorum as revealed in the physical embodiment of the rhetor); Warnick (2007), for instance, argues that the assessment of ethos must take place through the internal logic and design of an argument, rather than as attached to the arguer (who may not be revealed in many cases). Although such an analysis is useful, it focuses on the text (in the service of rhetorical analysis) and not on the writer. In contrast, Sherry Turkle (1995) posited that users (who write their identities into the virtual spaces they inhabit, from e-mail, to online discussion boards, to MUDs) could inhabit multiple identities in their online environments through a process of fragmentation.

The study of identity as a rhetorical construction also includes an interest in agency, as the digital realm has been characterized as both a space that frees one from control because it need not follow the metaphors and constraints of the physical world and one that exerts control through the establishment and enforcement of protocol (Galloway & Thacker, 2007). Contemporary digital rhetoricians are interested in the ways that hardware, software, and networks constrain online identity formation. For example, Kevin Brock (2010) notes that the "user who constructs an electronic identity (or many) is not the arbiter of that identity's boundaries; instead, it is the developer(s) of the relevant technology that have assigned the limits to what a user can be or do with that technology" (n.p.) and, in a similar move, Jennifer Bay (2010) examines "Web spaces in which bodies are 'tagged' and take on mediative properties that construct subjects. . . . Each site allows for certain kinds of cultural codes, which are invented and arranged by computer code and which function as the attributes or markup of the body" (154).

Bay's work in particular focuses on the ways that discursive markers of one's physical identity cannot be erased from the performance of online identity; in addition, there is an increased desire for more authentic markers of real bodies (such as through the use of video, webcams, and profile pictures). Bay's examples show that "the drive for real identity disadvantages women from being accepted as authentic or expert (blogging), constrains the types of bodies and connections that can be made in gendered terms (social networking and dating sites), and affects the ways that women can comport themselves toward others" (163–64). Bay's examples show a distinct connection between the body and digital identity (perhaps addressing, albeit not in a necessarily positive way, the concerns that Killingsworth raises about the erasure of the body in digital discourse). And, as Bay argues, "what we do online now requires there to be more continuity—or at least fluidity—between our online and off-line selves" (155).

Digital rhetoricians are also concerned with the ways in which race is constructed, marked, or elided in online communities. In "The Appended Subject: Race and Identity as Digital Assemblage," Jennifer González (2000) addresses the question of how "visual representations extend or challenge current conceptions of racial and cultural identity and relations of power" (29), using a rhetorical analysis of three sites that feature the body as a primary element to interrogate representations of the body-as-object, disassembled into individual elements. More recently, Lisa Nakamura's (2008) *Digitizing Race: Visual Cultures of the Internet* is a detailed study of representations of race online in a process that she articulates as "digital race formation" as she develops a method that can "parse the ways that digital modes of cultural production and reception are complicit with this ongoing process" (14).

Another area that I have begun to think about with regard to digital rhetoric is how identity, and by extension, agency (another critical consideration for digital rhetoric) can be enacted by nonhuman actors, as in the case of Bruce Sterling's "spimes"—as he defines them, a spime "becomes an instantiation of identity. It's named, and it broadcasts its name, then it can be tracked" (2005, 105); and it is in the tracking that spimes (as well as humans) leave traces of their identities, scattered throughout the network. The number of active software agents working on the Internet has increased dramatically as advances in artificial intelligence and the exigence of information overload (both in terms of quantity and speed) have necessitated the development of smarter tools for information acquisition, retrieval, and manipulation. The relationship between identity and network is not limited to software agents, however. A recent phenomenon is the rise of companies whose task it is to ensure positive online ethos for their clients. These companies, who provide "online reputation management" (Reputation.com, 2011), supply positive data points in the network and make sure these accounts appear higher on search engines than any negative ones do (and they also issue cease-and-desist letters to sites that they claim engage in defamatory practices, so they use a range of methods to accomplish their goal). In each of these emergent practices, the construction of identity is tied to the network.

Networks/Network Rhetorics

If the interface is the location and text most often addressed as the focal point of digital rhetoric investigations, it is the access to the network that such interfaces provide that has most fundamentally changed the way that digital texts use and enact digital rhetoric practices and principles. As Collin Brooke (2011) argues,

> The idea of the network has grown increasingly pervasive in recent years. Networks, as Alexander Galloway has written recently, function as allegorical indices for any number of intellectual, political, and/or social complex systems . . . we might ask ourselves if and how it might change the ways we consider rhetoric and writing. If indeed these perspectives represent a shift in our thinking, then a network(ed) rhetoric must be more than the ability to craft pithy status updates or the wherewithal to navigate privacy settings on Facebook. (n.p.)

Nodes and Links

Initial approaches to the concept of network used it primarily as a metaphor—borrowing the language of networking from graph theory, translating vertices and edges into nodes and links and connecting the idea of a network node to Barthes's (1974) term "lexia" (which he defines as "a unit of reading" [6]) in order to theorize hypertext (and, in particular, hypertext fiction) as constructed network.

Both "node" and "link" become important to digital rhetoric as they represent two rhetorical forms that are available for analysis, but it is the network itself that has become the more powerful form in terms of its affordances and constraints and the ways in which it mediates rhetorical situations, facilitates rhetorical ecologies, and impacts the formation of digital identity. In rhetorical terms, networks exercise power, and as Ulises Mejias (2008) argues, "networks—as assemblages of people, technology and social norms—arrange subjects into structures and define the parameters for their interaction, thus actively shaping their social realities" (qtd. in Langlois et al., 2009, 429). While the application of network theory has a long history in the social sciences (particularly in terms of social network analysis, covered in more detail in chapter 3), its use in humanities disciplines is relatively new. In 2004, a special issue of *JAC* focusing on complexity theory (which draws on network theories and methods) featured a number of articles that applied network theory to rhetorical theories and methods. Editors David Blakesley and Thomas Rickert (2004) asked authors to respond to Mark C. Taylor's (2003) *The Moment of Complexity: Emerging Network Culture*, suggesting that "Taylor's claims concerning our emergent network culture and its complex, adaptive logics challenge current postmodern and cultural theories while opening new faultlines in the established narratives of the humanities in general" (824). Byron Hawk's (2004) contribution to the issue begins by arguing, "The ancient civic space that led to the emergence of rhetoric has been replaced by contemporary network space" but that there are "few rhetorical theories that adequately address the complexities of this new social space" (831–32). Hawk suggests that a project to build a rhetorical theory based on the topoi of complexity and networks could begin by mapping the rhetorical terms of classical rhetoric to the vocabulary of complexity and network theory (which he proceeds to do, relating heuristics to schemata, the rhetorical situation to complex adaptive systems and reframing logos, ethos, and pathos as network, screen, and affect, respectively).

Tiziana Terranova's *Network Culture* (2004) presents a detailed overview of the network as rhetorical construct, which she frames as a network culture that is "inseparable both from a kind of *network physics* (that is physical processes of differentiation and convergence, emergence and capture, openness and closure, and coding and overcoding) and a *network politics* (implying the existence of an active engagement with the dynamics of information flows)" (3). A crucial move that Terranova makes draws on the larger understanding of networks as systems (not just technological but also biological and social) that can enact invention through their development: "If the network is a type of 'spatial diagram' for the age of global communication, the self-organizing, bottom-up machines of biological computation capture the network not simply as an abstract topological formation—but as a new type of *production machine*" (100, emphasis in original). The network then provides digital rhetoric with both theories and methods that address both analysis and production.

But rhetoric is concerned also with the question of power, and thus many digital rhetoricians have turned to Galloway and Thacker's (2007) theories of networks and network protocols to address the ways in which networks can simultaneously take on the roles of exigence and constraints (using Bitzer's [1968] terminology).

Protocol

Galloway and Thacker (2007) draw on the work of Deleuze (and, to a lesser extent, Deleuze and Guattari's *Thousand Plateaus*) to help identify and theorize the features of networks that function as forms of control, and, in turn, digital rhetoricians have made extensive use of Galloway and Thacker's theories (see Hilst [2010] for an approach that draws on both Deleuze and Guattari and Galloway and Thacker, filtered through an Ulmer-inspired lens). The main element of Galloway and Thacker's work that is taken up in rhetorical studies is the notion of protocol. In *The Exploit: A Theory of Networks* (2007), they focus on the issue of control, arguing that "networks, by their mere existence, are not liberating; they exercise novel forms of control that operate at a level that is anonymous and non-human, which is to say material" (5). It is from an analysis of the network's mechanisms of control (extending Galloway's previous theorization in *Protocol* [2004]) that they isolate and define the element of protocol, which "may be defined as a horizontal, distributed control apparatus that guides both the technical and political formation of computer networks, biological systems, and other media" (28).

Networked Publics

Featuring connections to both Terranova's network cultures/network politics and Galloway and Thacker's treatment of networks as the locations of geopolitical struggle, Langlois et al. (2009) focus on developing "networked publics" as an object of study for digital rhetoric; they suggest a "progressive departure from a focus on content . . . as the object of analysis to study the constitution of publics to consideration of the networked routes that assemble members of publics and connect them with issues" (427). This construction of a networked public holds promise as a framework for applying digital rhetoric methods and theories to large-scale social and media contexts, and it may be particularly useful when evaluating and intervening in power relations:

> We define networked publics as those publics that come into being through online informational processes. The online informational systems provide the material, communicational, and social means for a public to exist, and this takes place through the implementation of a network that defines the parameters of agency of a public and its specific communicative affordances. In that sense, the network provides the parameters for assembling issues and their publics in specific ways. . . . [T]he network can impose a specific communicative discipline at the same time as it can offer possibilities of re-articulation of preexisting power dynamics. (430)

Network Methods

Theorizing the network in rhetorical terms encourages the development of network-enabled methods, such as using the network as a model of context-specific relationships. Franco Moretti (2011) has taken up a network analysis approach to the study of literary texts (such as Shakespeare's plays); he argues that doing so allows for a different kind of analysis that leads to a different level of interpretation:

> Once you make a network of a play, you stop working on the play proper, and work on a *model* instead. You reduce the text to characters and interactions, abstract them from everything else, and this process of reduction and abstraction makes the model obviously much less than the original object—just think of this: I am discussing *Hamlet*, and saying nothing about Shakespeare's words—but also, in another sense, much *more* than it, because a model allows you to see the underlying structures of a complex object. (84)

However, a rhetorical approach to networks may require more complex approaches than simply using network analysis features to develop alternative models of different kinds of texts; in fact, the network itself may constitute an inventional force (which, when combined with the possibilities of software agents and digital texts exhibiting rhetorical characteristics independent of human direction, opens up an entirely new realm of challenges and possibilities for rhetorical theory). Terranova (2004) hints at this possibility when she suggests that we can conceive of the network "as a 'grand mesh,' a form able to accommodate all variation and its mutations—an abstract machine that goes beyond the model to become the actual terrain for the study and engineering of complex and innovative behaviours" (118).

Networks and Digital Rhetoric as Economies and Ecologies of Circulation

While I have thus far provided a broad overview and selected references to scholars who are applying, revising, or reframing classical and contemporary rhetorical theory in order to align it with digital rhetoric, I now turn to my own sketch of a digital rhetoric theory that is founded on principles of circulation. I have constructed this approach as both theory and method (which I call "circulation analysis"), so it serves to also bridge chapter 2: "Digital Rhetoric: Theory" and chapter 3: "Digital Rhetoric: Method." I begin by setting up a framework that situates digital circulation within specific ecologies and economies of production: while circulation ecologies represent the places, spaces, movements, and complex interactions of digital texts as they are produced, reproduced, exchanged, or used, the exchanges and uses that take place within those specific ecological circumstances are governed by the economics of circulation (which in turn are subject to the constraints and affordances offered by the situated ecologies in which the texts circulate).

Digital Ecologies

In one of his last works, Walter Ong suggested that

> The age in which humans existence is now framed, the age in which human life and technology so massively and intimately interact, can well be styled not only the information age and the age of interpretation, but, perhaps, even more inclusively, the ecological age, in principle an age of total interconnectedness, where everything on the earth, and even the universe, is interconnected with everything else, no only in itself but, ideally, in human understanding and activity. (qtd. in Walter, 2005, n.p.)

A scientific term originally applied to research on interactions in specific natural environments[2], "ecology" as a metaphor for complex, interconnected relationships has a rich history of use in writing studies (Cooper, 1986; Syverson, 1999; Nardi & O'Day, 1999; Spinuzzi & Zachry, 2000; Spinuzzi, 2003; Blythe, 2007). The basic scientific definition of ecology is "the study of the relationships of organisms to their environment and to one another. The key word is 'relationships.' Ecology is a study of interactions" (Brewer, 1988, 1); another key aspect of the science of ecology is the study of the ecosystem: ecology can be applied as the "ecology of the individual organism [or] the ecology of groups of individuals or populations," when taking the latter approach, it is important to acknowledge that "populations live together in communities—the community along with its physical setting or habitat is a single, interacting unit, the ecosystem" (11). Thus, the key elements of ecological study—relationships, interaction, complexity, and community—easily map onto qualitative studies of writing and rhetoric in both epistemological and ontological terms.

Ecology is also a useful framework for a theory of rhetorical circulation because it provides a systems-based view of both the environments and relationships that take place through digital circulation mechanisms. Systems are characterized by their compositions, environments, and structures (Bunge, 1979); in *Applied Systems Ecology*, Friedrich Recknagel (1989) explicates these systemic elements:

> The composition denotes the set of system components, the environment denotes the set of environment components which influence the system components. The definition of the composition and environment in turn implies the marking of the system boundary. The structure denotes the set of relations between composition and environment as well as within composition. (13–14)

Networks, particularly the digital networks in which digital texts circulate, are also systems, and in this way they can be similarly seen as elements in a digitally networked ecology of overlapping (and networked) ecosystems. Zan, Zambon, and Pettigrew (1993) argue that a "network is a system and not only a nexus of relations. Due to its systemic nature, a network is a working entity, which continuously reproduces its relationships and changes forms and contents over time. Therefore, networks are evolutionary systems, living organizations" (130); in other words, networks are ecological entities. The science of ecology uses this sense of system architecture to articulate its key unit of analysis: the ecosystem.

Ecologies and Ecosystems

Ecology as a field of study looks at both ecologies and ecosystems. Ecologies are internetworked and interacting systems made up of discrete ecosystems. An ecosystem can be "any size so long as organisms, physical environment, and interactions can exist within it" (Pickett & Cadenasso, 2002, 2), thus replicating the systems approach outlined above. As I use the terms, "ecology" is the super-structure and the theoretical lens; "ecosystem" is the specific system that a digital work originally belongs to when it is first distributed or published, but it is also the interconnected composition and environment that can be mapped and articulated through its circulation (and, indeed, that is one aim of circulation analysis).

Ecosystems represent specific, bounded locales where circulation takes place; and although circulation occurs across and through multiple ecosystems, the effects are best observed within particular localized systems; thus, ecologies represent the scales at which research on circulation may be most profitably undertaken.

Energy Flow and Material Cycling

Two important properties of ecosystems are that they have *energy flows* and they *cycle materials* (Kling, 2006); these two ecological properties can also be articulated as economic properties when applied to digital environments such as the Internet (indeed, Stephen Adler [1998] describes the Internet itself as an "information ecosystem"). In material ecosystems, such as ponds, forests, or oceans, the cycle of materials is enacted through the uptake, use, respiration, reformation, and reuse of the basic ecological components (e.g., plants, animals, water, carbon, nitrogen); the energy flows provide the engine for these material cycles though input and consumption (of solar/heat energy). These same essential processes can also be seen at work in digital production. The circulation of materials occurs in the use, remix, and appropriation of digital texts, and the energy that drives this circulation comes from the rhetorical activity of digital bricoleurs, often operating within particular social networks (in ecological terms, these are communities that inhabit specific ecosystems). In other words, the rhetorical activity of writers and the material labor of production is analogous to the input of energy per se into a natural system; once that energy (and the digital object that results from the deployment of that energy) is added to any given digital ecosystem, the interaction of environment (network) and other inhabitants (other digital texts) in that ecosystem generates relational links and instances of material cycling (also known as remix in terms of digital practice).

For example, YouTube (http://www.youtube.com), a digital video file-sharing service, allows users to post and circulate digital videos they have found or created. But a common practice in the YouTube community is to appropriate and reuse the materials that have been posted there. In some instances, the remix is not complex: simply adding subtitles to videos (as translations, or to add information, or providing a parody of the original content). Other videos represent more complex interactions: players of massively multiplayer online role-playing games (MMORPGs) such as *World of Warcraft* and

Guild Wars have created a number of music videos that feature choreographed in-game activity set to songs such as the Village People's "YMCA" or MC Hammer's "U Can't Touch This." For a particularly involved example, see YouTube user GraveDɪgger's "Guild Wars vs. World of Warcraft" (http://www.you tube.com/watch?v=YcWXL8jpFGs), which pits in-game choreography from two different MMORPGs as a dance contest set to Hammer's "U Can't Touch This" (which in turn samples Rick James's 1981 hit "Super Freak").

Cross-community *and* cross-media appropriation and circulation is fairly common in digital environments: in January of 2007, Clemens Kogler, Karo Szmit, and Andre Tschinder posted "Le Grand Content" to YouTube (http:// www.youtube.com/watch?v=lWWKBY7gx_0), describing it as an examination of

> the omnipresent PowerPoint-culture in search for its philosophical potential. Intersections and diagrams are assembled to form a grand 'association-chain-massacre'. Which challenges itself to answer all questions of the universe and some more. Of course, it totally fails this assignment, but in its failure it still manages to produce some magical nuance and shades between the great topics death, cable tv, emotions and hamsters. (n.p.)

The graphs and Venn diagrams that provide the content for "Le Grand Content" were originally published in Jessica Hagy's blog *Indexed* (http://indexed. blogspot.com), which features scans of diagrams that she draws on index cards.

But material cycling is certainly not limited to video production. Consider the case of Fark.com, whose users collect and aggregate headlines from newspapers and other online news sources, annotating them with amusing headlines; unlike the other examples, however, there is also an editorial mechanism that allows some headlines to be promoted to the main site while rejecting others—in ecological terms, this process may be understood as a "limiting factor," that is, an environmental factor that influences the maximum population of plants or animals in a given ecosystem.

Ecology as Metaphor

In describing circulatory activity as taking place within an ecological context, I draw on two approaches that also use the ecological metaphor: Nardi and O'Day's (1999) "information ecologies" and Spinuzzi and Zachary's (2000) "genre ecologies." Each of these formations plays a role in the structure of circulation ecologies, as both "information" and "genre" influence and are influenced by circulation, but I would suggest that information is too broad and genre is too narrow to effectively describe the interaction, movement, and exchange that occurs with the digital circulation of rhetorical objects. Information implies an object but does not incorporate use as an intrinsic component of that object's character. Genres shift and change not only over time but through the processes of circulation. What is useful, however, is the articulation of how both information and genres function within complex networks of interaction: how they interact within specific ecosystems.

Nardi and O'Day (1999) define an information ecology as "a system of people, practices, values, and technologies in a particular local environment. In information ecologies, the spotlight is not on technology, but on human activities that are served by technology" (49). This notion of information ecologies does two things particularly well: it shifts focus from technology as tool to technology-in-use (that is, activity can be seen as a synergistic relationship between digital media/technologies and human actors) and it focuses the lens of inquiry on a finite context (which is useful for the development of research methods). And I agree with Nardi and O'Day (1999) when they posit that "the ecology metaphor provides a distinctive, powerful set of organizing properties around which to have conversations. The ecological metaphor suggests several key properties of many environments in which technology is used. An information ecology is a complex system of parts and relationships" (50). They go on to provide an extended metaphor, taking into account habitations, niches, speciation, and other biological components of an ecological framework; but for my purposes, the two most important elements of the ecological metaphor are that "an information ecology is marked by strong interrelationships and dependencies among its different parts" (51) and that "locality is a particularly important attribute of information ecologies" (55).

Strictly speaking, what Nardi and O'Day (and later Spinuzzi and Zachary) term "ecologies" are actually ecosystems: ecologies are the larger contexts in which these individual ecosystems reside and interact. And while Nardi and O'Day have established perhaps the most well-known use of an ecological lens for rhetorical practice, their insistence on locating "ecologies" in specific material locations (such as libraries, schools, and hospitals) actually places artificial boundaries on an ecological perspective, thus robbing it of a fully realized vision of interconnectedness and interrelationships that occur through both local and global environments. The other drawback to Nardi and O'Day's approach to applying an ecological metaphor is that they disassociate the ecological view from the systems-level view (despite the fact that ecology is essentially a study of biological systems); if "the technological system is the water we swim in, and it has become life-sustaining and almost invisible to us" (43), then occupying a position within a particular ecosystem (or, more accurately, multiple ecosystems) and larger ecological structures is no less an invisible framework—until it is articulated and applied.

Spinuzzi and Zachary (2000) begin with the information ecology metaphor and extend it to their own work with what they call "genre ecologies." As they define it, a "genre ecology includes an interrelated group of genres (artifact types and the interpretive habits that have developed around them) used to jointly mediate the activities that allow people to accomplish complex objectives. In genre ecologies, multiple genres and constituent subtasks co-exist in a lively interplay as people grapple with information technologies" (172), and they argue that genres "are not static forms; they are dynamic, organic, and messy. To account for variations across instantiations of a given genre, a more robust, ecological perspective is required, one that accounts for the dynamism and interconnectedness of genres" (173). It is in this same vein that I therefore argue for an ecological perspective with respect to circulation in order to account for the dynamism and interconnectedness of rhetorical processes and the economics of production and circulation of digital work.

Whereas Nardi and O'Day's notion of information ecologies helps to frame the overall interaction between people, texts, and digital networks, Spinuzzi and Zachary's work on genre ecologies provides a description of how genres interact within specific ecosystems.

Circulation takes place both within and across specific, situated ecosystems; as I have noted, these ecosystems can be described in terms of the specific interactions between people, texts, and technologies. Thus, any method for examining or researching circulation must take into account not only the actors, networks, and interactions but also the specific articulation of media and technology within those networks. Ecosystems, then, have rhetorical, technical, and social dimensions that influence the possible routes of (and interactions made possible by) circulation; these ecosystems can be framed as networks within specific and situated institutions (such as a department within a university or workplace), but they can also be framed in terms of digital spaces that are bounded by genre and activity. For example, eBay represents a particular ecosystem that engages a specific form of trade that is framed by eBay's interface, user communities, and system of ratings. Similarly, communities of users form networks within Flickr's social networking and image-sharing system that do not correspond to networks outside of the Flickr ecosystem (although there are connections across and through other networked ecologies). Some digital systems are also tied to specific user networks, such as posting links to del.icio.us that serve a particular course at a specific institution; in these cases, there is a connection between local (physical) communities and public digital networks; the intersection of local use and public digital spaces represents an important area of inquiry for the study of circulation.

Ecological systems as I see them can also be articulated in terms of scale (that is, the methodological lens can be focused narrowly or widely): digital ecologies can be identified as micro-ecologies (as in the work/portfolio of a single individual), midrange ecologies (which contextualize the work of collaborators, departments, research groups), or macro-ecologies (institutions, fields, disciplines, nations).

Economies of Circulation

If "ecologies" represent the contexts of circulation, "economies" represent the mechanisms that motivate circulation, primarily through the process of production, distribution, and exchange (using Marx's terminology). The key to how and where a given text will circulate is based upon the value of that text, which can be assessed in terms of either use-value or exchange-value. Because Marx's work is concerned with material production, his framework includes consumption as an integral (and cyclical) component of the production process (and also required for the establishment of value). Consumption, however, becomes useful only at a metaphorical level when the object of the exchange is digital: exact reproductions can be made that do not consume the original products. Consumption can be described in terms of external resources (such as the living expenses of the scholar(s) who develop digital texts), but it no longer plays a direct role in the economies of circulation (although one might substitute "use" for consumption in order to fulfill all of the requirements of production in Marx's theory). This is not to say that digital objects are immaterial—they have material value by virtue of use and exchange. But it is useful here to depart from a strictly Marxist interpretation of capital and consider the role of what Bourdieu calls "cultural" and "social" capital in the economies of circulation.

It is important to note at the outset that I am *not* using Marx's notion of circulation here, because his use of circulation is both limited in scope and is divorced from production (which is the opposite of my contention that, rhetorically speaking, circulation plays an important role in all of the classical rhetoric processes, from invention to delivery). In his "Introduction to a Contribution to the Critique of Political Economy," Marx states both that "circulation is merely a particular phase of exchange or of exchange regarded in its totality" and that "exchange is simply an intermediate phase between production and distribution" (*Capital*, II: 203). This view of circulation is particularly limited as well since Marx asserts that "circulation time and production time are mutually exclusive. During its circulation time, capital does not function as productive capital, and therefore produces neither commodities nor surplus-value" (*Capital*, II: 203). Because Marx would say that circulation adds no use-value, and therefore no surplus value, the limitation that I see here is the insistence on separating the processes of production and circulation (the "time" part of the equation).

Marx's view of capital itself is closer to my use of circulation, as he describes capital as "a movement, a circulatory process though different stages, which itself in turn includes three different forms of the circulatory process. Hence it can only be grasped as a movement, and not as a static thing" (*Capital*, II: 185). Patrick Murray (1998) argues that capital is indeed "not a thing, and not a historical constant, but a bizarre and astoundingly powerful (asocial) social form of wealth turned 'automatic subject'" (37). Murray's odd turn of phrase in declaring capital an "(asocial) social form of wealth" seems particularly apropos when applied to circulation—it invokes both the human activity that motivates circulation as well as the independent work of both human and nonhuman actors that facilitates the paths and mechanisms of circulation. Murray goes on to say that "the circulation of capital involves not simply a flow of materials but metamorphoses, *a flow of forms*" (37, emphasis in original); substitute "digital texts" for "capital" and this neatly describes my description of the process of circulation in digital communication networks.

Marx does recognize that circulation "is just as necessary for commodity production as is production itself, and thus agents of circulation are just as necessary as agents of production" (*Capital*, II: 205), but again, his theory is grounded in material production, thus requiring a kind of translation into a form that might be useful for understanding economies of circulation. Marx notes that transportation adds value (and surplus value) because it affects the use-value of commodities: "the use-value of things is realized only in their consumption, and their consumption may make a change of location necessary, and thus also the additional production process of the transport industry" (*Capital* II: 266–67). One might reframe this for digital networks: circulation (transportation) adds value because digital texts can be appropriated (although not consumed); this kind of use increases use-value, although the real change wrought by digital circulation is always better expressed as exchange-value (which is possible without having to include consumption as a necessary component of production or necessary outcome of distribution). And this reframing shows where I must most sharply disagree with a Marxist interpretation of circulation. As Murray explains, "no value and, *a fortiori*, no surplus value is created in the restricted sphere of circulation for a simple reason: in this sphere no use-value is (preserved or) added to the commodity, and if no *use-value* is (preserved or) added, no *value* is added. For, while a use-value need not be a value, value depends on use-value" (46, emphasis in original). I would contend that circulation is the principle mechanism not only for enabling exchange-value but also for adding use-value to the rhetorical object via its reproduction, appropriation, and use within a particular circulation ecology or through interactions across multiple circulation ecologies.

Circulation makes the rhetorical object available for appropriation, thus increasing the use value. Consider the case of the MA thesis that is bound and sent to a university library—the thesis is in circulation, but its form severely limits the scope of said circulation, as its ecology of use is bound to the physical space it can occupy. That same thesis, made available on the web, is much more likely to be read, quoted, and cited—that is, to garner increased use-value. The rhetorical object itself is in essence a "flow of forms."

The production of digital objects endows them with use-value, but the motivation for production is grounded in the subjective exchange-value that is garnered through the distribution and publication (and ultimately circulation) of the texts. Because digital circulation does not function in the same way as material production, it is better to approach the question of exchange-value not through Marxist theory but via Bourdieu's theory of cultural capital. Particularly in terms of scholarly work and knowledge management ecologies, digital objects are not typically traded for material or monetary gain; instead, the exchange-value of the work comes from the accrual of cultural or social capital.

Bourdieu's (1977) project began as an attempt "to extend economic calculation to all the goods, material and symbolic, without distinction, that present themselves as rare and worthy of being sought after in a particular formation—which may be 'fair words' or smiles, handshakes or shrugs, compliments or attention, challenges or insults, honour or honours, powers or pleasures, gossip or scientific information, distinction or distinctions, etc." (178); my own interest in developing an economics of circulation would fall in with the latter categories of symbolic goods, as I am particularly interested in the kinds of formation (genres) that occur in academic settings. In a sense, the Marxist perspective can be used to consider the circulation of digital texts as capital that requires labor, production, and distribution, while the Bourdieu-ian perspective is concerned less with the object of circulation and more with the composers and appropriators of those texts.

Economies of circulation, then, must account for both the use-value and exchange-value acquired by rhetorical objects as they circulate through digital networks as well as the social capital these works are exchanged for by their authors and appropriators. As with circulation ecologies, these processes are complex and interdependent, relying on the relationships between human and nonhuman actors who are connected via digital networks.

THREE

Digital Rhetoric: Method

In addition to addressing the roles and activities of the speaker/writer, communication/text, and audience/reader, definitions of rhetoric that address digital communication need to account for context, interactivity, and circulation (via internetworked systems). Lloyd Bitzer's (1968) articulation of rhetoric as "a mode of altering reality, not by the direct application of energy to objects, but by the creation of discourse which changes reality through the mediation of thought and action" (4) provides a useful starting point for digital rhetoric by virtue of being an abstraction that does not explicitly address or evoke specific practices or media associated with rhetorical production while simultaneously acknowledging the power of rhetoric as a meaning-making activity. Hauser (1986) provides a more streamlined general definition of modern rhetoric as "the management of symbols in order to coordinate social action" (3); for both Bitzer and Hauser, rhetoric is an activity and not just an analytic framework.

In the case of the definitions I draw on above, none of the theorists address the complications of digital circulation or the possibilities of nonhuman agents becoming rhetorical actors. And while Hauser acknowledges that symbolic modes need not be constrained to the verbal, he does not address these other modes in his work (moreover, it is important to understand how multimedia and multimodality function at the intersection of multiple symbolic modes, and how this might complicate the "management of symbols"). Digital rhetoric, then, should take into account the complications of the affordances of digital practices, including circulation, interaction, and the engagement of multiple symbol systems within rhetorical objects, and its methods need to explicitly engage those complications and affordances.

Because I situate my professional identity at the same nexus as the point of origin for digital rhetoric as a field of study, I see composition/rhetoric, computers and writing, and professional writing as the fields that best understand how to research rhetoric and writing, and by extension, that provide the most effective starting points for assembling digital rhetoric methods. In this chapter, I will first address the traditional rhetorical method of close reading and the relatively new inverse of that method, which Franco Moretti (2000) calls "distant reading." I then cover the methods from fields in writing studies and then go on to examine methods from fields that do not take rhetoric as their theoretical or methodological foundations.

Close and Distant Reading as Rhetorical Methods

One of the most widely employed rhetorical methods is close reading. Close reading as a technique promoted by I. A. Richards (1930) focuses upon meaning within the text as it is evidenced in formal qualities (such as rhythm, use of imagery and metaphor) as interpreted by the reader; in this version, the text is considered apart from the author, its cultural or historical context, or the material conditions of its construction; as Edwin Black (1965) notes, the aim is to determine "the purpose of a text from evidence the text itself provides" (16). Taken up as a foundational methodology by the New Critics in literary study, it has since shifted from methodology to method (i.e., technique) and the term has taken on the broader meaning of attentive reading in the sense that its formal qualities are reflections of social and historical effects and that the text itself may deploy rhetorical power outside of its internal interpretation. Barry Brummett (2010) defines close reading as "the mindful, disciplined reading of an object with a view to deeper understanding of its meanings" (3). It is in this sense that close reading, which Brummett connects to paying attention to the implicit contributions of the text to sociocultural effects (such as privileging a particular language over others) that is of the most use to digital rhetoric. The practice of engaging the formal qualities of a text can also be useful, but in this case "text" must be read in the comprehensive sense outlined in chapter 2 and the formal qualities would include those specific to different media (which may be disaggregated within the process of close reading for critical interpretation).

It may seem obvious that close reading or textual criticism is available as a method, but it has such strong ties to print text that I want to be sure that it does not lose ground as a method for digital text, particularly given the lengthy arguments that situate digital text as distinct from print text and my subsequent arguments that we need to develop digital-native methods for born-digital texts. Close reading, in the sense of applying our individual faculties to the interpretations of any given text, will nearly always be in play as an undercurrent of other methods.

But close reading also serves as a starting point because it provides the contrast for newer rhetorical methods; one of these, distant reading, can be seen as a natural opposite in terms of technique—rather than bounding the text and looking only at what it offers, distant reading takes a long view, examining the text as one among many and considering a much larger corpus whose contexts and relationships give rise to different forms of meaning. Franco Moretti's (2000) practice of "distant reading" sees distance as "*a condition of knowledge*: it allows you to focus on units that are much smaller or much larger than the text: devices, themes, tropes—or genres and systems" (57, emphasis in original). Distant reading methods require computational processes whose output is presented as specific forms of data visualization to dramatically alter the scales at which readers encounter texts (Mueller, 2009). Moretti (2005) examines the employment of three types of data visualization applied to large-scale corpus of literary texts: graphs, maps, and trees, and Derek Mueller (2009) adds clouds as an additional distant reading visualization (more on tag clouds appears later in this chapter, when I consider data visualization as method). One of the focal points of this chapter is to encourage synthesis and development of new methods for digital rhetoric, just as Moretti combined computational analytics and data visualizations in order to develop a new method for literary study—but also to encourage the extension of extant methods, as Mueller has done with Moretti's work.

Research Methods in Writing Studies

New texts on research methods in writing studies (including Bazerman [2007] and Hughes & Hayhoe [2007]) for the most part don't include digital methods. Individual scholars have been pushing for new methods that take into account the role of digital production in rhetorically centered research methodologies (see, for instance, Spinuzzi [2003], Spinuzzi & Zachary [2000], and Hart-Davidson [2005], discussed in more detail below, as well as Swarts [2008] and Potts [2009]), but fewer researchers in composition and technical communication are focusing on tools and methodologies that arise from the rhetorical functions of the digital network itself.

Composition as a discipline is currently undergoing a significant shift in its overall focus: as composition continues to engage multiple modes and media as acceptable forms of composition (beyond the tradition of print-based writing), the practices and processes of composing that composition takes as its object of inquiry are undergoing radical changes—changes that necessitate concomitant changes in research methods. These changes amount to what is essentially an epistemological shift from a view of the solitary writer who has available only limited material means of production and often no recourse to distribution or circulation of the work, to a view of composition as a collaborative activity that engages multiple means of production and that occurs within digital networks that provide broad opportunities for publication and circulation.

The research methods in professional writing and technical communication tend to lend themselves more readily to the discovery of agents interacting in writing ecologies; Laura Gurak and Mary Lay's *Research in Technical Communication* (2002) contends that the foundational research methods in professional writing are "ethnography, textual analysis, historical research, survey and questionnaire research, and experimental work" (vii). The methods of professional writing, like composition/rhetoric and computers and writing, tend toward the qualitative, although the field is more accepting of quantitative methods and experimentation. Historically, professional writing research has paid more attention to context (particularly in terms of organizations and workplaces) than other writing studies research traditions.

Two of the key research traditions from professional writing that are particularly appropriate for digital rhetoric are genre studies and usability.

Genre studies, as elaborated in professional writing research, focus on investigations of "an individual's repertoire of situationally appropriate responses to recurrent situations" through examinations of the "situated actions of writers and the communication systems in which those . . . actors participate" (Berkenkotter & Huckin 1995, ix). In methodological terms, genre studies privileges a multilayered approach that engages both micro- and macro-level interactions. As Berkenkotter and Huckin explain,

> . . . what microlevel studies of actors' situated actions frequently depict as individual processes, can also be interpreted (from the macrolevel) as communicative acts within a discursive network or system. Genre is the concept that enables us to envision the interpretation of process and system in disciplinary communication. (ix–x)

This approach to the study of writing processes and practices is particularly useful when applied to digital environments, which engage individual and collaborative practices that take place within both digital and discursive networks. Focusing the lens on the activity of the writer or the context (and its conditional affordances for composing) allows a view that collapses system-centric and user-centric activity.

Another methodology that is especially well-suited to the study of digital composition is usability. Usability is not well understood as a rhetorically based qualitative research methodology outside of the field of professional and technical communication; more often than not, it is equated with observing users performing tests of preset activities under controlled conditions and is typically seen as *developmental* (i.e., typically developing information tools, interfaces, and systems), and not as a research methodology at all. However, if usability is rearticulated as a method of investigating actual use in specific contexts and cultures, it is clear that it can be a powerful method for understanding rhetorical knowledge-making activity within a broad range of contexts and uses. As I've written elsewhere (Eyman, 2009),

> To engage usability as a suitable methodology for studying writing processes and pedagogies, it's important to first acknowledge that writing is a technology, and, consequently, that teaching writing is part of a technological system; a system with which our students interact as users. Constructing students as users allows us to see them not as subordinate to the learning process, but as engaged participants in the technological system that is bounded by the institutions, departments, and physical spaces in which learning activities take place. Students have particular needs and goals, but we don't always have a clear understanding of what those needs and goals are from the perspective of the user; curricular design is all too often enacted through a systems-design framework, rather than a user-centered framework. (222)

Usability, in other words, provides a methodology for studying both writing practices and writing pedagogies—and because it takes both system and user into consideration, it provides appropriate methods for studying digital writing practices and digital pedagogies.

Digital Writing Research

While many traditional research methods in composition/rhetoric and professional writing—particularly qualitative research practices—will continue to function well regardless of the material conditions of production, new methods need to be developed to help us better understand how composing practices change from traditional print production activities to multimodal, multimedia productions that can now be delivered, distributed, published, and circulated in and through digital networks.

The general trend of research in composition/rhetoric and professional writing toward qualitative methodologies works well for the study of digital compositions because it takes into account situation, context, and media. Case studies, textual inquiry, and rhetorical analysis are particularly useful for investigations of rhetorical activity in digital environments, although in each case there is room for enhanced methods that can be adapted for use in digital networks. While the methods currently available cover quite a bit of ground in terms of researching digital writing practices, there are a few areas for which appropriate methodologies have not yet been developed, as well as a series of emerging methods that show a great deal of promise.

New methods include systems of visualizing discrete elements in the writing process as it takes place between and among multiple composers/authors. Hart-Davidson, Carter, and Sun (2006) suggest that producing different views (visual representations) of particular compositional and communicative activities can support different frames of analysis. This methodology is tied to a revision of the nature of composition as a rhetorical practice, as they assume "that writing is a medium, and that people are more often users of texts (as opposed to participants in a conversation); writing is not the focus of the action, but a powerful context for action" (20).

Shifting the research paradigm from a study of writing-as-action to writing-as-context allows for the development of new methods that might help us better see how this approach to the use of writing may be investigated. William Hart-Davidson's (2005) work on establishing a rhetoric of objects, relationships, and views is an example of how context, system, and user might work well as the focus of inquiry for writing-as-context.

In the past decade, there have been few works that address digital, networked writing in terms of research methods—many articles and book chapters have explored the way that literacy changes when it takes place in digital contexts, how teaching must change to be successful for online courses, or have provided examples of new media practice—but the general consensus seems to be that we can apply traditional rhetorical, genre, or discourse analysis methods regardless of medium or context. In 2007, however, editors Heidi McKee and Dànielle DeVoss published the first collection that explicitly addresses methods for digital writing research: *Digital Writing Research: Technologies, Methodologies, and Ethical Issues.*

McKee and DeVoss (2007) define "digital writing research" as

> research that focuses: (a) on computer-generated, computer-based, and/ or computer-delivered documents; (b) on computer-based text-production practices (and we deploy *text* broadly here, to include multimedia artifacts); and/or (c) on the interactions of people who use digital technologies to communicate. . . . Further, the term digital writing research—rather than the more commonly used term *Internet research*—acknowledges that not all digital writing and related communicative acts and interactions occur on the Internet. (3)

Digital Writing Research is an important collection for a number of reasons: it represents an acknowledgment of the broadening scope of what counts as writing activities—as James Porter notes in the foreword, "the chapters in *Digital Writing Research* show us, either implicitly or explicitly, that the definition of "writing" has changed in the digital age and that, consequently, our approaches to doing research need to change; we need a parallel and equally dramatic change in our notions of methodology" (xiii). But the collection also represents a starting point for a disciplinary engagement with digital research methods for writing studies that has the potential to bring into sharp relief the kinds of theoretical and methodological shifts that must happen when writing moves from print to digital in nature. As Porter argues in the foreword:

> Likewise, digital writing research should not be viewed merely as research about writing with technology. It should be viewed, rather, as changing the fundamental assumptions about methodology, particularly the humanist assumption that divides the human from the technological. Digital writing research takes a cyborgian view and a networked view of human communications. It is not simply old methods applied to new events or practices. It represents a new way of looking altogether—an approach that emphasizes the role of production, delivery, and technology in human communication, but even beyond that, acknowledges the hybrid, symbiotic relationship between humans and machines. (xv–xvi)

While many of the approaches that appear in *Digital Writing Research* contribute to a rhetorical reconfiguration of the specific methods I examine below (and will thus be addressed within the contexts of those methods), the works by Kevin DePew and Julia Romberger in *Digital Writing Research* together provide a framework within which all of the following methods may be employed.

DePew (2007) argues for the importance of triangulation—of looking not just at texts but at contexts and users. He suggests that, "as rhetoricians, we should be examining more features of the communicative situation rather than merely an artifact it produces. What else can we learn about digital rhetoric when we also study the rhetor's intentions? The audiences' response to the text? How local contexts shape this interaction? . . . In essence, I am advocating that digital rhetoric researchers adopt strategies framed by the communicative triangle—the rhetor, the audience, the digital text or discourse, and the contexts. By designing such methodological strategies, researchers insert communicative participants into the process, which gives researchers the opportunity to see both the complex nature of the research site and apertures in the field's tropes" (52). I would add that the communicative participants need not be solely human audiences, but may be elements of the networked digital systems themselves (indeed, Jason Swarts [2008] provides an example of how nonhuman discursive agents may be included in technical writing research methods).

Romberger's (2007) work similarly focuses on context but addresses it within an ecological metaphor:

> An ecofeminist methodology, in short, must be aware of context and its complexity—the ecology of the situation. It is this emphasis on the influence of environment upon subjects in an ecological ebb and flow and how these relationships are articulated that separates it from other feminist methodologies. It takes into account histories of the larger social milieu and remains aware of the context of the researcher and the system of values brought in by framing an inquiry in a specific theory and discipline" (250).

Taken together, these two positions—engaging context and expanding the scope of research methods to include the textual, the social, and the rhetorical situation—provide a platform for digital rhetoric research. But before such a platform can be fully articulated and deployed, the methods that work within it must be identified and, in some cases, developed. In the remainder of this chapter I review research methods from a broad range of fields and disciplines that may be profitably appropriated for digital rhetoric research.

C.O.D.E. and Network Administration Tools

If rhetoricians are to develop methods that are "digital-native," then looking to the tools and metrics that run these digital environments, such as network and routing tools and the protocols upon which the Internet was built, would be a logical first step. Even though digital texts are themselves immaterial, the networks in which they reside are made of physical data conduits and routing devices. When I worked as a webmaster and systems administrator for a community college, I learned about a variety of tools that were designed to monitor the health and productivity of these networks: I could keep track of how many hackers were attempting to infiltrate my servers or how robust the network link between two buildings was on a moment-by-moment basis. Although I know of several technorhetoricians whose backgrounds include experience in systems administration or programming, the first to articulate a coherent method for using these network tools for digital writing research is James Ridolfo (2006), who developed a webtext evaluation suite that he called "C.O.D.E.—Comprehensive Online Document Evaluation." Ridolfo presents this suite of tools as a pedagogical application that students can use to "not only cite online documents, but also critically research . . . digital texts."

Ridolfo provides instruction on using three network analysis tools to un-cover both geographies and owners of digitally networked systems, along with two additional web-based tools for examining the changes over time that a given website experiences. The "geography and ownership" tools that Ridolfo discusses include whois, traceroute, and ARIN. When I first learned to use tools like traceroute, the only way to do so was via the com-mand line (usually on another server, although these tools are available on all personal computers as well). However, web-based interfaces for these tools have been developed—making the tools themselves more accessible to students and researchers alike. The first tool in C.O.D.E. is called "whois." Whois (http://www.betterwhois.com) allows the user to retrieve informa-tion about who has registered a domain name, including date of registra-tion, administrative contacts, and billing addresses. Traceroute, the second tool in C.O.D.E., traces the route that an Internet request must travel to reach its destination. For instance, when you use a web browser to view a page such as http://www.msu.edu, your browser sends a request from wher-ever you are to the server that hosts that site; this request travels through the various hubs and routers that lay between your computer and the server at Michigan State University. Traceroute reinforces the geographic nature of interconnected networks and generally shows the overall distance between two networked points. The output of traceroute also shows the names of the routers and systems it encounters, so you can learn which Internet Service Provider (ISP) hosts the server at the end of the trace. Ridolfo argues that "these two utilities allow us to . . . contextualize the website based on its geographic origins, 'publisher' (ISP), time, and new authorial information" (n.p.). The final tool in the C.O.D.E. suite is ARIN—American Registry for Internet Numbers (http://www.arin.net)—which allows users to look up the registration information of Internet addresses. So, for instance, ARIN re-ports that the IP address 35.8.10.26 belongs to Michigan State University and that MSU's ISP is Merit Network Inc.

The other techniques covered in C.O.D.E. help the user to find out more about the *web-based* (as opposed to the physical network-based) context of a given site. Using the Web Archive (http://archive.org) allows the researcher to access previous versions and edits of many websites. The original website for the online journal *Kairos: A Journal for Teachers of Writing in Webbed Environments* (which was renamed *Kairos: A Journal of Rhetoric, Technology, and Pedagogy* and changed web addresses in 2001) is available by searching for the original web address (http://english.ttu.edu/kairos) in the Web Archive; the archive also provides links to all of the versions and updates that have taken place since then. The final activity in C.O.D.E. is a Google search of the URL for the site under consideration. Searching for the URL (as opposed to the site name or content) provides a quick view of the role this site has in the larger discourse of online communities (however, it is not as powerful a tool as cataloging the links to that site from other sources, a technique that is discussed in the section below on bibliometrics and cybermetrics).

Because digital communication can be deceptively ethereal, these tools help to recover the underlying material structures of the digital networks we study; additionally, these methods also reveal the activities of the nonhuman actors in the system, such as the routers that carry and promote the network's communication signals and the servers that respond to the queries initiated by people or other servers.

Studying Web Usage via Server Log Analysis

A great deal of information about users of digital genres (such as blogs, wikis, or websites) can be found in the log files automatically generated by the servers that house digital texts. These logs record how a user's search strategy leads to a particular text, and how many individuals have accessed a given text. Server log analysis can show which pages are entry points for users and which are exit points, how many times a given page is viewed, how many "unique users" have visited a site, and some basic information about where those users come from. It is possible to combine server log analysis with the use of cookies or content-management system supported sites to track how long users spend on a given page and what paths a user takes when moving through a site (server logs can also record what link or search engine result lead a user to a site's entry point, although it typically does not have access to the search query).

Server log analysis yields very basic quantitative data that can show how a specific site's traffic has changed over time, as well as some characteristics of a site's audience. Examining the server logs from the online journal *Kairos*, for instance, provides a picture of a steadily growing number of accesses over the past decade, as well as an increase in international audiences:

> In addition to the steady increase in overall readership, we've seen a shift from a primarily US audience to a much more international audience. A little over 80% of our readers come from the US, which means that about 20% come from elsewhere—the logs have recorded visitors who hail from 190 different country codes, from Belize, Belarus, Botswana and Brazil; from Vietnam, Venezuela, and the Ukraine. And that 20% is now over 9,000 readers—so I'd say it would be safe to consider *Kairos* an "international" scholarly publication venue. (Eyman, 2006)

Although server log analysis is limited, it can serve as a starting point for understanding the relationship between a given digital text (or context) and its audiences. Additionally, server log analysis provides data that can be used to help triangulate findings from other methods. Server log analysis is tied to circulation analysis because it can provide a general picture of the number of individuals accessing a digital-native text and also provide some information about where those individuals are from. However, this kind of overview should be considered secondary information because it does not directly connect the digital texts to its users and uses. One significant drawback of server log analysis, however, is that the researcher needs to have access to the server logs themselves—and this kind of information resource is rarely made public.

Social Network Analysis (SNA)

Because of its focus on networked relationships and their support of the circulation of social capital, Social Network Analysis (SNA), a research approach from sociology and communication science, provides a powerful set of tools for digital writing research. Social network analysis focuses on patterns of relations among people, organizations, states—in other words, human relationships, but rarely human/nonhuman interactions or relationships (Wellman & Berkowitz, 1988; Scott, 1991; Wasserman & Faust, 1994). Social network analysis takes a mixed-method approach: SNA makes use of qualitative data gathered via interviews, surveys, observation, and artifacts (Rogers, 1987; Garton et al., 1997), but it uses quantitative analyses to interpret that data. As Lin Freeman (1997) notes,

> From the outset, the network approach to the study of behavior has involved two commitments: (1) it is guided by formal theory organized in mathematical terms, and (2) it is grounded in the systematic analysis of empirical data. It was not until the 1970s, therefore—when modern discrete combinatrics (particularly graph theory) experienced rapid development and relatively powerful computers became readily available—that the study of social networks really began to take off as an interdisciplinary specialty. (n.p.)

The basic premise of social network analysis is that relationships cannot be discretely quantified as units of measurement; that is, the relationship between two individuals must always be seen within the context of all the other relationships those individuals engage in (either shared or separately). This approach presents a high level of complexity that is handled by statistical analysis and the mathematical formulas that describe networks in terms of nodes and ties; as Joseph Barnes (1972), credited with being the first researcher to study social networks, explains, "to discover how A, who is in touch with B and C, is affected by the relation between B and C . . . demands the use of the network concept" (3).

In social network analysis, nodes represent the individual actors within networks; ties represent the relationships shared by those actors—these relationships (also called "strands") can be described in terms of content (the resource that is exchanged), direction, and strength. Some network analysts have applied social network methods to electronic texts, using SNA tools to surface patterns of relations between words and phrases; however, unlike the kind of mapping that similar work in applied linguistics produces, SNA textual analysis is used to "reveal cognitive maps and identifies people who hold similar conceptual orientations" (Garton et al., 1997, n.p.).

Social networking analysis methods have been used to trace the circulation of social capital (Ooka & Wellman, 2003; Huysman & Wulf, 2004) and thus are particularly well-suited to questions of digital economies and circulation: as Barry Wellman (2003) notes, "Networks are a major source of social capital mobilizable in themselves and from their contents" (n.p.). The work that social analysts do focuses on tracking and tracing the movement of resources between people; they "seek to describe networks of relations as fully as possible, tease out the prominent patterns in such networks, trace the flow of information (and other resources) through them, and discover what effects these relations and networks have on people and organizations" (Garton et al., 1997, n.p.).

Several researchers in rhetoric and writing have begun adapting social network analysis methods for studies of online interaction that are based on writing practices; these methods, however, are event-based rather than relationship-based (Hart-Davidson, 2007).

Hypertext Network Analysis (HNA)

Hypertext Network Analysis (HNA) is, in a sense, a form of social network analysis, but it moves the question of relationships away from people and organizations and instead looks at the nodes and ties of digital texts as instantiated in websites and web links. The key distinction between social network analysis and hypertext network analysis is that the websites themselves are considered actors within the networks being investigated: "In particular, through a hyperlink, an individual website plays the role of an actor who could influence other website's trust, prestige, authority, or credibility" (Park, 2003, 53).

Park and Thelwall (2003) argue that "compared to other Web methods such as a content-based analysis, the relative advantage of hyperlink analysis is that it is able to examine the way in which Web sites form a certain kind of relations with others via hyperlinks" (n.p.)—thus the hypertext link serves as the focal point of the investigation. Hypertext link analysis also tends to be applied to very large-scale data sets. Broder et al. (2000), for instance, examined two hundred million pages and 1.5 billion hyperlinks in a study that showed that the probability of a hyperlink path between two randomly chosen Web pages was about 24 percent. When a path was present, there was an average of approximately sixteen hyperlinks in the path between pages. These kinds of topological investigations take advantage of network analyses in ways that are similar to those of Ridolfo's C.O.D.E. suite of networking tools, but they use only the explicit links among and between websites to uncover the connections between them.

Hyperlink analysis has also been applied as part of the methods available to cybermetrics, drawing on Rousseau's (1997) analogy between citations and hyperlinks (coining the term "sitation" to foreground the similarities). As Park and Thelwall (2003) note, "the analogy between hyperlinks and citations has continued to generate interest within information science, including speculations about the kind of information that they could reveal in different contexts" (n.p.). This connection of citation and hyperlink also evokes the circulation of social capital, as both hyperlinks and citations can be indicators of (and can be mapped as) social/academic capital forms of resource exchange.

Bibliometrics and Cybermetrics

The most obvious (and traditional) method of tracing the use and value of texts is through citation analysis, although its use is limited when considering the overall circulation of a text. Still, as Kaplan and Nelson (2000) point out, "in the absence of a more compelling metric, citation analysis remains the best commonly available indicator of usage" (324).

Citation analysis as a process and a field of study provides numerous means and methodologies for use in quantifying a record and history of citation for authors, articles, and journals. The simplest method of citation analysis is to select a time frame and a body of citation data and determine how many times an author, article, or journal has been cited by the publications indexed in the dataset within that time frame. In most cases, citation data for this sort of bibliometric analysis is drawn from citation databases, such as Social Sciences Citation Index (SSCI), Science Citation Index (SCI), and Arts and Humanities Citation Index (AHCI), which are all accessible online from Thomson's Institute for Scientific Information (ISI) database, also known as the Web of Science.

Scholars also employ citation analysis methods called co-citation and author co-citation in order to map disciplines (Small, 1999; White & McCain, 1998), determine subfields within major areas of study (Bayer, Smart, & McLaughlin, 1990), and locate cross-disciplinary influences (Small, 1999). The raw data included in co-citation analyses of articles, journals, and authors includes the number of times that pairs of articles, journals, and/or authors are co-present in the works cited or footnotes of articles located through citation databases. As Bayer, Smart, and McLaughlin (1990) explain, co-citation assumes "that the more frequently two scientists are cited together, and the more similar their patterns of co-citations with others, the closer the relationship between them" (444). This kind of relationship can be viewed as an instance of circulation activity that can be directly tracked. The problem of utilizing bibliometric methods for examining circulation (both print and digital) is that the databases are not complete—they are selectively populated both in terms of the works and citations they track and by a calculation of value (in terms of academic capital) that is applied to those works based on the citations they receive from other works that already have an established value. Thus the scope is very limited in terms of an overall picture of knowledge production and circulation.

Of course, qualitative methods of citation analysis are also employed in order to determine how authors incorporate citations and the ideas of the texts they cite within their scholarship. Such analyses require examining the use of citations within scholarly texts to determine the rhetorical functions of those citations (Budd, 1999; Hyland, 1999). Budd's (1999) study of internal citations in seventy sociology articles from 1990 to 1995 reveals that authors use most of their citations quantitatively, also called procedurally in Budd's terminology, in order to prove to readers that they thoroughly researched their respective topics and are aware of disciplinary contexts (271). As Budd notes, procedural citations, those not integral to knowledge claims made by the authors, outnumber epistemic citations by a ratio of more than three to one (271). Authors' use of citation in largely procedural ways supports our assertion above that the citation of particular materials reflects and reinforces the significance of those items as important texts in the field that must be taken into account and acknowledged by authors as a condition for the perceived credibility of their arguments, even if the references cited are not integral to their arguments. On the other hand, items that are not cited can be viewed as having less credibility and may be judged as largely irrelevant.

A more promising method for digital writing research can be located in new informetric methodologies—based in part upon the principles and statistical formulas developed for bibliometric analyses—that are being developed by researchers in the field of information science. Several terms for these new methodologies have been suggested, but the field currently appears to favor "cybermetrics" as the designation for the study of online scholarship.

Cybermetrics studies the network of links between electronic scholarly works, revealing how widely a specific electronic source is linked to other online texts, what types of texts link to specific sources, and how the source is used. Aguillo (2003) locates cybermetrics at the intersections of "cyber-geography" and "cyberdemography" across Internet genres (such as e-mail, the World Wide Web, and online databases). Methods include adaptations of bibliometrics, user studies, calculations of "cyberindicators" (website hits, search engine rankings), assessment of web data architecture and hyperlink topologies, and comparative search engine analyses.

Initial research on web linking began with bibliometric approaches, but it soon became apparent that new methodologies would need to be developed in order to study the web from an informetrics perspective: Larson (1996) used linking as an analogous method of citation analysis to devise a map of the intellectual structure of cyberspace; Kleinberg (1999) demonstrated that useful information about individual web pages and websites can be extracted directly from link structures; and Broder et al. (2000) asserted that hyperlinks themselves can be studied as objects of interest in their own right.

Content Analysis

Content analysis is the systematic, quantitative analysis of communication content (including verbal, visual, print, and electronic communication). According to C. W. Roberts in the *International Encyclopedia of the Social and Behavioral Sciences* (2001), "content analysis is a class of techniques for mapping symbolic data into a data matrix suitable for statistical analysis" (2697); in this regard, content analysis is similar to social network analysis, except that it focuses on the representations in and across individual texts rather than the relationships between them. List (2005) makes clear that content analysis, "though it often analyzes written words, is a quantitative method. The results of content analysis are numbers and percentages. After doing a content analysis, you might make a statement such as '27% of programs on Radio Lukole in April 2003 mentioned at least one aspect of peacebuilding, compared with only 3% of the programs in 2001'" (kya16a.html).

Content analysis is typically applied in one of two general modes: conceptual analysis or relational analysis. Conceptual analysis establishes the existence and frequency of concepts—most often represented by words or phrases—in a text; in contrast, relational analysis examines the relationships among concepts in a text (Busch et al., 2005).

Busch et al.'s (2005) description of relational analysis echoes the call for understanding relation complexities that occur in social network analysis, where the individual ties have no meaningful relationship except within the context of the larger network:

> Relational analysis, like conceptual analysis, begins with the act of identifying concepts present in a given text or set of texts. However, relational analysis seeks to go beyond presence by exploring the relationships between the concepts identified. Individual concepts, in and of themselves, are viewed as having no inherent meaning. Rather, meaning is a product of the relationships among concepts in a text. (n.p.)

There are two forms of relational analysis that hold promise for digital writing research: proximity analysis and cognitive mapping. Proximity analysis, like co-citation analyses in bibliometrics, looks for the co-occurrence of concepts in the texts being studied. In text-based proximity analysis, the concept takes the form of a string of words. Cognitive mapping uses the results of a proximity analysis and displays them as a visual map that represents the relationships between concepts (this is, indeed, very similar to the sociograms of social network analysis, which provide maps of relationships between people or groups). Busch et al. (2005) enumerate the theoretical assumptions that support this kind of mapping: "mental models are representations of interrelated concepts that reflect conscious or subconscious perceptions of reality; language is the key to understanding these models; and these models can be represented as networks" (n.p.). These kinds of maps are difficult to create by hand; like the mathematical approaches employed in social network analysis, the development of concept mapping for content analysis has been greatly aided by advances in computing—in other words, the digital environment itself is necessary to support these methods. Early proponents of concept mapping describe it as "a computerized multidimensional scaling technique that generates maps of content themes based on the frequency and co-occurrence of key words" (Miller & Riechert, 1994, 3).

One example of content analysis applied to digital writing research is Herring et al.'s (2004) "Women and Children Last: The Discursive Construction of Weblogs," in which the authors use content analysis techniques to assess the age and gender of weblog authors:

> Gender of blog authors was determined by names, graphical representations (if present), and the content of the blog entries (e.g., reference to "my husband" resulted in a "female" gender classification, assuming other indicators were consistent). Age of blog authors was determined by

information explicitly provided by the authors (e.g., in profiles) or inferred from the content of the blog entries (e.g., reference to attending high school resulted in a "teen" age classification). (n.p.)

Herring et al. also used a content analysis rubric to develop type categories for the weblogs themselves, dividing them into "filters," which primarily feature links to world events, online happenings, and other nonauthor-centered issues; "personal journals," which primarily contain the blogger's thoughts and internal workings; and "k(nowledge)-logs," which are "repositories of information and observations with a typically technological focus" (n.p.). This second move is a rhetorically-informed variation on traditional content analysis techniques, which often do not take into account the context of the texts under consideration.

In our chapter in *Digital Writing Research*, Colleen Reilly and I utilized a similar form of content analysis to develop a heuristic for evaluating digital texts in terms of their structure, the digital environments in which they reside, and the degree to which they violate traditional print-based genre norms (Reilly & Eyman, 2007). Drawing on Bolter and Grusin's (1999) theories of remediation, we examined the content of electronic scholarly publications to determine their degree of departure from the conventions of print texts and the extent to which they exploit and even highlight the affordances, structure, and multimedia nature of texts native to digital environments. We established a continuum that includes four designations for electronic texts: highly transparent, moderately transparent, moderately hypermediated, and highly hypermediated (Reilly & Eyman, 2007). In order to code the websites that we examined as falling into these categories, it was necessary for us to consider not only textual content but also paratextual content (links, document structures) and the kinds of visual and interactive content that can be published on the web. Thus, our work is also an example of how content analysis techniques can be applied to both textual and visual elements in digital texts.

Data Visualization

Composition/rhetoric as a field is experiencing a renewed interest in the role of the visual, particularly as it is used in multimedia and multimodal compositions; professional and technical writing has long understood the importance of visual rhetoric for effective communication. The "turn to the visual" also plays a prominent role in digital research methods, particularly in the form of data visualization.

Visualization is not simply a tool for displaying the results of analytic methods; it is itself a method that can be used to structure data in ways that reveal patterns—in other words, it is an analytic technique in its own right. Lengler and Eppler (2007) define visualization methods as "systematic, rule-based, external, permanent, and graphic representations that depict information in a way that is conducive to acquiring insights, developing an elaborate understanding, or communicating experiences" (n.p.). In their "Periodic Table of Visualization Methods for Management," Lengler and Eppler divide visualization methods into six distinct groups: data visualizations (visual representations of quantitative data in schematic form); information visualization (interactive visual representations of data designed to amplify cognition by transforming the data into an image that is mapped to screen space); concept visualization (2-D graphical displays where concepts are connected by directed arcs encoding brief relationships between pairs of concepts); metaphor visualization (which first positions information graphically to organize and structure it and then conveys an insight about the represented information through the key characteristics of the metaphor that is employed); strategy visualization (which uses complementary visual representations to improve the analysis, development, formulation, communication, and implementation of strategies in organizations); and compound visualization (a mix of any of the foregoing visualization types).

An example of data visualization used methodologically is Kichiyoshi et al.'s (1999) "Data visualization for supporting query-based data mining," which describes how visualization can help users test hypotheses about the structures and contents of databases with which they are interacting. In their method, "an instance in a database which has several attributes with numerical or nominal values is visualized as a color bar with several color parts which correspond to attribute values. Values of a function which evaluates the utility of a hypothesis are also visualized by using colors. This visualization technique helps users find an initial hypothesis and modify the hypothesis in order to increase the usefulness of it interactively" (888). Like this and other examples, most applications of data visualization as research method come from quantitatively oriented disciplines, such as the use of sociograms in social network analysis and hypertext network maps in hypertext network analysis.

Data visualization is very useful for making accessible large-scale systems that might not otherwise be comprehensible. As Roger Brown (1965) explains,

> Social structure becomes actually visible in an anthill; the movements and contacts one sees are not random but patterned. We should also be able to see structure in the life of an American community if we had a sufficiently remote vantage point, a point from which persons would appear to be small moving dots. . . . We should see that these dots do not randomly

approach one another, that some are usually together, some meet often, some never. . . . If one could get far enough away from it human life would become pure pattern. (165)

Applying the functionality of a concept map coupled with a frequency analysis of terms that appear in the journal *College Composition and Communication*, Derek Mueller (2007) has implemented a system that visually represents the main themes of each issue in the form of a "tag cloud."

Tag clouds can be generated automatically by extracting the most common phrases from a given corpus (as with the example above), or they can represent the tags that individuals apply to content in folksonomic systems. In either case, this form of data visualization has clear potential as a digital rhetoric method.

Complicating Factors for Digital Research Methods

Although each of the preceding methods can, I believe, be adapted, appropriated, and synthesized for use in digital rhetoric research (after infusing them with a rhetorical foundation and vision), there are several complicating factors that will affect any method used for digital writing research. The main factor (and the one from which the others derive) is access. Accessibility can be impeded by intellectual property gatekeeping (restricted access to networks and texts that circulate in and through those restricted systems, as well as cost-prohibitive access fees on certain content), but it is also an issue when considering the format of the rhetorical objects themselves. Digital texts can be made up of, in part, proprietary formats; they may also engage media or genres for which we currently have few (if any) tools that would allow us to fully understand how they work or their relationship to their digital environments. Finally, the problem of ephemerality is also endemic to digital texts: websites are not stable entities that are fixed (they are unfixed by their very nature), and many become inaccessible by ceasing to exist. As noted above, some sites are still recoverable via the Web Archive, but this is not always the case: Colleen Reilly has recently alerted me to the fact that the Web Archive now retroactively obeys no-index restrictions placed in robots.txt files, meaning that any site that adds that directive to a new version will cause all past versions to go dark in the archive. Quite a number of academic institutions and departments are applying these no-index controls (the rationale for doing so is unclear), which means that they are effectively erasing their histories from the network. Clearly, any digital-native methodology must be aware of how these issues of access and control constrain the methods that are used.

FOUR

Digital Rhetoric: Practice

This final chapter focuses on three main areas of digital rhetoric as practice: pedagogy (teaching digital rhetoric), publication both about and instantiating scholarship of digital rhetoric, and examples of digital-rhetoric-in-action in the production of multimodal, new media, and other networked, digital texts.

Digital Rhetoric and Pedagogy

The power of rhetoric lies not just in its analytic or productive capacities, but in its emphasis on pedagogy. If we can build effective theories about how to use and construct digital media for the accomplishment of persuasive enterprises, we can also teach those theories and the rhetorical practices derived from those theories. Classical rhetoric, the starting point of my project, is deeply concerned with teaching; from Protagoras's insistence that the art of persuasion can be taught to Quintilian's codification of the pedagogy of classical rhetoric, every explication of rhetorical theory has included a pedagogical foundation. This, too, is why rhetoric is best suited for developing a framework of understanding for digital media. Robert Coover (1999) neatly sums up the importance of rhetoric to digital production and pedagogy:

> Rhetoric, in this Age of the New Sophists, is still the route to power, but the hypertextual link and all the visual and aural media are now part of its grammar. Like composers, artists, and filmmakers before them, writers will learn to battle through the new tool-learning tasks, or to collaborate with other artists, designers, filmmakers, composers, and the tools themselves will become easier to learn and use and will interact more smoothly with other tools. (n.p.)

One of the first projects that I worked on as a graduate student at Michigan State University was an article on teaching digital rhetoric that was produced by a collective that we alternately called DigiRhet.org or DigiRhet.net (I favored the latter, but in our first publication, the attribution is listed as the .org variant). The idea for the formation of the group (and much of the content of our first publication) came from the first Digital Rhetoric graduate course at MSU, taught by Dànielle DeVoss. We published "Teaching Digital Rhetoric: Community, Critical Engagement, and Application" in the spring 2006 issue of *Pedagogy* (the collective subsequently published "Old+Old+Old=New: A Copyright Manifesto for the Digital World" in the summer 2008 "Manifesto" issue of *Kairos*, but I was not one of the authors on that project). As the title indicates, our approach to teaching digital rhetoric focused on three key elements that we felt were foundational—understanding and developing a sense of community (as it is engaged both online and in the classroom itself), a focus on critical engagement with the technologies of production and delivery, and a method for developing facility with the applications that support the production of digital texts.

Our approach specifically addresses rhetoric as both analytic and heuristic for production; we argued that "digital rhetoricians must explore both theory *and* technology; critical engagement alone is just as insufficient as a curricular approach as would be practical application without the provision of tools for understanding how technologies work within social and cultural contexts" (249).

While I believe that the DigiRhet framework has value, it is not the only approach to teaching digital rhetoric—other approaches range from teaching multimodal composition and web design from a digital rhetoric perspective to focusing on the theories and methods that constitute the field (aligned with the theories and methods I have described in previous chapters). I have chosen three courses that take different approaches to teaching digital rhetoric to show how these differences might play out depending on whether the focus is on the theories that undergird digital rhetoric or engaging in the development of digital texts using digital rhetoric as a methodology. The courses I have chosen are Sarah Arroyo's graduate Seminar on Digital Rhetoric, taught in spring 2009 at California State University, Long Beach; Byron Hawk's undergraduate Advanced Writing—Digital Rhetoric course taught in fall 2010 at the University of South Carolina; and my own undergraduate course on Web Authoring and Design, taught in spring 2011 at George Mason University. These are of course not the only approaches to teaching digital rhetoric, and many other examples are available.

Sarah Arroyo: Seminar on Digital Rhetoric

Arroyo's course syllabus begins with an overview and brief definition of digital rhetoric that is aligned with the definition I finally arrive at in chapter 1:

Digital rhetoric has irreversibly infiltrated our lives, and so it deserves intense scholarly attention beyond simply acknowledging that more people write and communicate with computers. Digital rhetoric entails more than critiquing writing we encounter in digital environments or producing simple web texts; instead, studying digital rhetoric requires examining theoretical and ideological issues involved in the shift from writing in a text-only medium. Accordingly, digital rhetoric does not just mean that more people write with computers or that more people are online; rather, it entails larger cultural shifts in recognizing new patterns of thinking, rethinking familiar conceptualizations about both the self and human interaction, and re-envisioning attitudes and expectations toward reading, writing, and rhetoric, regardless of the physical presence of machines. (1)

Each of the courses presented here asks students to use rhetoric for both analysis and production. Arroyo's syllabus states that

digital writing performs and analyzes and critiques. Instead of only critiquing digital culture as is usually done by writing academic papers, we will critique digital culture within the medium itself. We will be introduced to a set of theoretical problems put forth mainly by Roland Barthes, Giorgio Agamben, and Greg Ulmer. We will work through these problems by creating short projects. We will then perform the theories we study by making short digital movies and/or web-based multimedia projects. (1–2)

Examining the reading list for the course, I noticed that readings in classical rhetoric and those that specifically invoke digital rhetoric (such as Warnick's [2007] *Rhetoric Online*)—with the exception of Zappen's (2005) TCQ article—were not included; rather, Arroyo focuses almost exclusively on contemporary rhetorical theory (including postmodern and poststructuralist approaches) combined with a number of readings on social networking, YouTube, and new media (the majority of which are freely available online—a common feature of many digital rhetoric courses since there are so many examples and approaches that are available on the Web and published in open-access journals such as *Kairos* and *Vectors*).

The absence of readings in classical rhetoric is not a weakness; Arroyo clearly situates her approach as one that works through the lens of cultural studies, which she specifies in the first course objective listed on the syllabus:

Upon completion of the course, you should be able to apply both traditional cultural studies practices (critiquing our consumption of digital writing spaces) and emerging digital studies practices (participating in the production of digital writing spaces) and discern rhetorically appropriate ways to do so. (5)

Both Arroyo and Hawk use the Ning platform, which allows users to quickly and easily set up a shared social networking site where participants can upload text (blog posts), images, and video. Ning also includes built-in integration with Facebook, Twitter, and YouTube. The incorporation of a social networking aspect into the course follows the DigiRhet recommendation of providing ways for students to experience (not just critique) online community as a key feature of digital rhetoric practice. Arroyo requires students to engage each other through online discussions, thus emphasizing the social aspect of networked discourse.

The other aspect of the course that resonates with the DigiRhet recommendations is the importance placed on producing digital texts (rather than only on traditional seminar papers) as the main product composed by students in the course. Arroyo asks her students to complete two short projects, each of which includes both a written argument and a version of that argument presented in a digital medium ("audio, video, web-based, or a combination"). The larger product for the course is a multimedia project (which may consist of multiple media, but the coursework appears to promote video as the default option). The multimedia project's instructions begin with the following description:

> This video or multimedia presentation will grow from your work in the course and will respond to a set of issues raised in the readings. You can think of it as a "postcritical" object, rather than the usual critical essay we write in graduate seminars. This will not be a critical analysis of the texts we read, but instead will be a performance of your responses to them. It will take on the same topic you address in your seminar paper and will "argue" by way of a different medium. (7)

Students also produce a twelve- to fifteen-page seminar paper that accompanies the project; Arroyo provides the rationale for engaging in both new media and traditional print literacies in the course by noting that "we are living in a time on the cusp where traditional literate practices are still highly valued" (7); I have yet to encounter a digital rhetoric course whose products are only new media, but I believe that the perspectives gained by using the more familiar critical approaches in print literacy to reflect upon, analyze, and critique digital rhetoric production are a beneficial pedagogical practice and I hope that we do not shift to purely nonprint-media works in such courses as long as print literacy is still a dominant mechanism for knowledge production in our society.

Byron Hawk: Advanced Writing—Digital Rhetoric

Byron Hawk's course is at once similar to Arroyo's (particularly in terms of the use of a class-based social network and the focus on digital text composition as the main product of the course) and also a bit different in terms of its theoretical focus. Because this is an advanced undergraduate course, there are far fewer readings, and most of those are less formidable than the theory texts required in Arroyo's course (although both Hawk and Arroyo draw on work by Gregory Ulmer—for Arroyo, there are several required readings; for Hawk, *Internet Invention*, which is a suggested reading on Arroyo's syllabus, is one of the key required texts). However, Hawk's main divergence is the focus on rhetoric (rather than cultural studies) as the primary disciplinary lens (evidenced in part by his use of Warnick's *Rhetoric Online* as the first required text listed on the syllabus). The course description reads (in part):

> Since the emergence of the Internet in the early to mid nineties, attempts to understand its impact on writing and rhetoric have shifted almost as fast as new software, hardware, and social worlds have come onto the scene. This means that any understanding of digital writing is always in process and understood through the process of participation and production. This class will discuss some key rhetorical concepts in relation to digital spaces, explore those concepts in the contexts of blogging and social networking, and then give students the opportunity to engage those concepts through a final digital writing project of their own.

Students in the course use Ning for a class-based social network, although they are encouraged to investigate and participate in other, real-world social networks as well. An element of play is also present in the use of Ning, as Hawk explains that students will "participate in the network via blog posts, forum discussions, real time chat, and posting found content from the web. Each week I'll post some kind of assignment on the syllabus or announce it in class and we'll hack around in the network after class discussions." In previous versions of this class, Hawk had also required students to post "vlogs"— video blog posts—as response to course materials.

Like Arroyo's course, Hawk's features two shorter projects (one of which is a traditional paper while the second includes print, multimedia, or video options) and a primary media project. Although he keeps open a number of possibilities for the media project, the main description states

> For the final media projects, students can select a web site, blog, or video format. . . . In class we will be studying a particular rhetorical approach

to these projects and doing small assignments along the way that can be built into the final project. Each media format has its limits and possibilities that you may not be able to completely anticipate ahead of time. So, I would choose the technology you are least familiar with (so you can have a chance to learn it) or that might suit your future needs (so you can learn more about it).

Douglas Eyman: Web Authoring and Design

Unlike Arroyo's and Hawk's courses, my course shifts attention away from theories and critiques of digital rhetoric and focuses almost exclusively on production (which is not an unexpected departure; unlike the courses above, which are designed to study digital rhetoric explicitly, my course is essentially a course in web design). I include it as an example here because I teach principles and practices of digital rhetoric as foundational elements for website production, but I situate such principles as intrinsic and embedded in the design activities themselves rather than as theories or methods to be studied independent of the lived experience of making a digital text.

In contrast to the extensive descriptions provided by professors Arroyo and Hawk, mine is relatively brief:

> Web Authoring and Design provides a rhetorical foundation for web authoring and design in professional settings. Students will learn basic principles of writing for the web, information architecture, coding for accessibility, and usability testing. The production-oriented component of the course provides instruction in writing valid code and practice with web- and graphic-editing software tools.

I also apply digital rhetoric as a framework both implicitly and explicitly (although in the latter case identified simply as "rhetoric") in the course goals and objectives:

> We will approach authoring for the World Wide Web from a variety of perspectives:
> We will look historically at patterns and trends that have shaped the Internet and the web and how these patterns and trends characterize the web today.
> We will look critically at how individuals, businesses, government organizations, and others construct and distribute knowledge within and through electronic spaces.

We will look rhetorically at a variety of web sites to better understand effective and not-so-effective web design and to identify trends in digital design and information architecture.

We'll learn to apply rhetorical principles as both heuristic and method for the design of websites. We'll explore design as a key element of web authoring. And we'll learn to code XHTML and CSS.

We will then apply these principles and practices by designing our own web spaces (working in raw code as well as composing with website editors), and by capturing, creating, and manipulating graphics. And, most importantly, by reflecting upon and writing about the choices we make as we select among available technologies and approaches to perform web-authoring tasks.

The majority of the coursework consists of completing a series of design and coding activities; the focus on rhetoric occurs in course discussion and site critique (which draws on both classical rhetoric and visual rhetoric/design principles for critical analysis). There are relatively few readings in theory, rhetoric, or other digital studies, although when I teach the course with a technical communications focus, I include Chanchu Lin's (2007) "Organizational Website Design as a Rhetorical Situation" and Kevin Hunt's (2003) "Establishing a Presence on the World Wide Web: A Rhetorical Approach." The main course text is *The Elements of User Experience* (2011) by Jesse James Garrett.

Garrett presents a web design and development process that engages five "planes":

- the strategy plane, which focuses on product objectives and user needs
- the scope plane, which addresses functional specifications and content requirements
- the structure plane, which considers interaction design and information architecture
- the skeleton plane, which focuses on interface design, navigation design, and information design
- and the surface plane, which applies sensory design (primarily visual for web sites)

In the course, I map these planes to the considerations of classical rhetoric, where the strategy plane connects to audience (user needs) and purpose (product objectives), the scope plane (invention), the structure and skeleton plane (arrangement), and the surface plane (visually representing ethos, pathos, and logos). We also address questions of memory (storage, site hosting, whether to allow indexing and archive in webarchive.org) and delivery (circulation, accessibility of flash objects, HTML 5 versus XHTML, and search engine optimization) through class discussion and online examples.

From my perspective, I see this course not as a study of digital rhetoric but as using digital rhetoric for specific kinds of digital text production. In the next section, I'll examine a similar pair of approaches as expressed in published scholarly work that either examines digital rhetoric practices or enacts them as part of the scholarly argument.

Digital Rhetoric Research and Scholarship

Examining digital rhetoric scholarship as practice means not just looking at research on digital rhetoric but also highlighting the publication of scholarly work that is presented as digital text, utilizing digital rhetoric to craft the research itself within the framework of new media. To that end, after a brief review of selected works that are published in traditional print journals, I provide a series of examples of scholarly webtexts. These are drawn from *Kairos* because, as editor and publisher, I am most familiar with what is available and I can speak to the productive work that went into creating these examples— but also because there are relatively few venues that publish peer-reviewed scholarship in digital-native formats (*Enculturation*, *Fibreculture*, *Vectors*, and *Computers and Composition Online* are some of the other journals that support such digital-native scholarship in rhetoric and writing studies).

Scholarship of Digital Rhetoric

Depending on what "counts" as digital rhetoric, a literature review of traditional scholarly works would be quite extensive; since I do cast a very wide net in terms of what falls under the purview of digital rhetoric, rather than compile an exhaustive list of works, I will instead provide a selection, first highlighting the approaches singled out in Zappen's (2005) catalog of digital rhetoric scholarship and then providing an overview of recent work that exemplifies a range of methods and objects of study for digital rhetoric research.

Jim Zappen's (2005) "Toward a Digital Rhetoric" article (which, paired with Lanham's [1993] "Digital Rhetoric and the Digital Arts," serves as the impetus for my own interest in digital rhetoric) focuses on four main areas: refiguring rhetorical traditions for digital texts, defining characteristics of new media, developing digital identities, and forming online communities. Zappen provides three to four examples of work in each of these areas. What is interesting is that he sees the work of digital rhetoric as taking up rhetorics of technology as well as taking technological invention, process, and text as the object of study. For instance, the first example he uses is Laura Gurak's

(1997) examination of rhetorical proofs at work in two online debates that focus on then-new technologies and their effects on users. While Gurak's analysis is on the function of ethos (in particular) in online debate, it is both an investigation of the character of the discourse within the context of digital media and a consideration of the rhetorical moves deployed by the technology makers and marketers.

Zappen also draws on Gurak's (2001) work as an example of the move to catalog and define the characteristics of new media. Gurak identifies speed, reach, anonymity, and interactivity as key elements of digital communications (features that Ian Bogost [2007] critiques as "subordinate" rather than primary processes, as speed, reach, and anonymity "simply characterize the aggregate effects of networked microcomputers" and Gurak's use of interactivity is a "vague notion of computer-mediated discussion and feedback" [25]). Zappen also cites Anders Fagerjord (2003), who doesn't so much focus on understanding the characteristics of new media as to suggest (drawing on Bolter and Grusin [1999]) that they synthesize the characteristics of previous media in a process he calls "rhetorical convergence." Fagerjord issues an early call to draw on interdisciplinary methods (in addition to close reading) to better understand digital texts: by reading such texts "with the concept of rhetorical convergence in mind, we become aware of the constant mingle of rhetorical forms inherited from earlier media and acknowledge as well the emergence of new communicative ways enabled by computer technology" (319).

For the final two elements, identity and community, Zappen provides a very brief gloss of his examples. The only work he cites that focuses fully on identity is Sherry Turkle's (1995) *Life on the Screen: Identity in the Age of the Internet*, and the consideration of community-building looks only at social networking researchers—in both cases, there were a number of works that focused on identity and/or community formation (a number of which appear in Taylor and Ward's [1998] *Literacy Theory in the Age of the Internet*, for example, not to mention Howard Rheingold's work on virtual communities [1993] and "smart mobs" [2002]).

The value of Zappen's call to consider the development of digital rhetoric lies not in the abbreviated literature review that he provides but in the categories of work in digital rhetoric (which serve as a usable framework for identifying what kind of work qualifies) and in his suggestion that digital rhetoric could be theorized and framed as a field of inquiry.

Finally, I will round out this overview with a brief review of more recent work that has appeared in *Computers and Composition* (the print journal of the computers and writing field) and *New Media & Society* (the print journal of Internet research studies). My first two selections focus on the concerns and questions of building community in online networks (as one of the key practices of digital rhetoric), but each takes a different methodological and disciplinary approach.

Christian Pentzold (2010) studies how Wikipedia authors understand and articulate "community" by examining online discussions among editors and applying a grounded theory approach to the analysis. Pentzold concludes that the Wikipedia community sees itself as an "ethos-action community" that follows a specific ethic that has developed through shared practice. He notes that his study "shifts the focus from structural criteria for communities to the discursive level of community formation" (704). While rhetorical theories and methods are not explicitly invoked, the outcome (which is a well-understood construction of community within rhetorical studies) arrives at a rhetorical conclusion. Pentzold's use of grounded theory can itself be seen as a rhetorical method, and he notes that "the analytical process unfolded as flexible accessing, sampling, structuring, linking, tentative conceptualizing and reviewing that resulted in the empirically grounded theory of the ethos-action community of Wikipedia authors" (716); in other words, a rhetorical construction that arises from his investigation. At the level of theory, this work would certainly have benefitted from a rhetorical approach to community and to ethics. The detailed structural framework that he develops (and the visualization of the "discovered network of categories" [713] produced by the study), however, shows that the methods he is using would certainly be useful to the study of digital rhetoric as well.

In contrast, Giuseppe Getto, Ellen Cushman, and Shreelina Ghosh (2011) approach the question of community from a new media composition perspective that is rooted in rhetorical understandings of community and identity. And rather than examine a community as an outside observer, each author provides data from communities they worked in and in which they functioned as both researchers and digital text composers, creating a video that profiles a local neighborhood center, a digital installation on the history of the Cherokee Nation, and a digital project focused on the preservation and practice of Indian classical dance amid its remediation via new media technologies. They use these case examples to "explore a model of community mediation that is cognizant of the practices and structures of communication within a given community. This model also acknowledges the boundary between the definition of community identity and the possibility of connection to both internal and external audiences" (160).

While very different in approach, both this article and the one by Pentzold examine community in ways that may well be complementary. Each of these works certainly stand alone and do not require the application of additional methods, but I would suggest that there are opportunities for researchers coming from different perspectives to work together under the auspices of digital rhetoric (and, of course, I am claiming both articles as instances of digital rhetoric scholarship—regardless of the disciplinary perspective of the authors—because the focus is on digital community formation).

Another area of continual development in digital rhetoric research focuses on methods and methodologies. In "Towards a Mediological Method: A Framework for Critically Engaging Dimensions of a Medium," Melinda Turnley (2011) draws on Régis Debray's development of mediology as an interdisciplinary method to develop a framework specific to new media production from a writing studies perspective. She notes that Debray's system "can help us account for both the conceptual and material aspects of media at both the macro levels of cultural structures and the micro levels of practice. Its emphasis on intersections between praxis and ideology can inform critical analysis of media artifacts and discourses as well as authorial decisions about media composition" (126). Turnley's appropriation and application of such a methodological framework to the analysis and production of digital texts is one of the practices that digital rhetoric can engage when developing new theories and methods. As she explains,

> Inspired by this approach, I have developed a framework for analyzing media specifically within the context of composition studies. This framework includes seven dimensions—technological, social, economic, archival, aesthetic, subjective, and epistemological—which are particularly relevant to media's functions as cultural formations and sites of rhetorical praxis. (126)

She then goes on to show how this framework can be applied as a generative (as opposed to definitive) rubric for the assessment of digital texts and performances (and those that cross digital/physical processes, such as flash mobs that are organized via Facebook but enacted in specific "real-world" locations). What is interesting about this approach is that it would lend itself very well to the kind of coding, analysis, and visualization undertaken in Pentzold's (2010) grounded theory approach to the development of community in Wikipedia.

Finally, one of the more interesting recent developments in digital rhetoric is a renewed interest in digital economies as rhetorical structures. Richard Lanham (2006) in *The Economics of Attention* suggests that rhetoric (and specifically the rhetorical canon of style) can support a new economic model that depends on acquiring and maintaining the attention of the audience in order to accrue economic value (in terms of monetary as well as social capital). James Porter (2010) believes that Lanham's view of rhetoric is not broad enough—

that "a broader view of rhetoric would include inquiry procedures (that is, inventional tactics) aimed at understanding what motivates people to create, search, and circulate knowledge" (174). In "Rhetoric in (as) a Digital Economy," Porter argues that economics has always been an important component of rhetoric and that "rhetorical contexts themselves rely on an economic system of exchange . . . an exchange of value that serves as the motivation for the production and circulation of digital objects" (174). Porter examines a range of social networking interactions in terms of their economic activity and suggests that there are a range of ethical concerns (access, control, labor exploitation) that must be addressed by designers of interactive systems (this approach is reminiscent of Kreiss, Finn, & Turner's [2011] Weber-inspired examination of the relationship between peer-production and bureaucratic control systems). The connection between digital economies and digital rhetoric is a productive space for continued digital rhetoric research, and I will finish with Porter's argument for the appropriateness of making that connection:

> . . . is it possible that rhetoric can help shape and influence the digital economy and social networking? My answer to that question can be summed up in two phrases: "information" and "knowledge work." If the basis of a digital economy concerns (a) the development of "information"—and not just information as a static product, but more important the transformation of information into useful knowledge; and (b) if the digital economy concerns the delivery and circulation of information via social networks in ways that create value for users, then writing teachers, communication scholars, and rhetoric theorists certainly have a lot to offer this discussion. (190)

While there is a broad range of very exciting work being done in digital rhetoric, what I find even more encouraging is the possibility of developing not just new theories and methods but new forms of scholarship that can take advantages of the affordances of new media digital texts—that is, scholarship *as* digital rhetoric. Christopher Basgier (2010) applies the dual lenses of author-function (a la Foucault) and genre-function to examine three digital-native scholarly texts in order to examine "how scholarly webtexts construct and respond to the very problems they themselves manifest: the relationships and differences between print and digital texts" (157). Basgier finds that scholarly webtexts "mobilize ownership and transgression, multimodal complexity, and multivocality as significant, valued practices in new media scholarship" (157)—and it is to such practices that I turn as I consider some key examples of digital-native scholarly webtexts.

Scholarship *as* Digital Rhetoric

As the editor and publisher of *Kairos: A Journal of Rhetoric, Technology, and Pedagogy*, I have had the pleasure of watching (and in some respects, participating in) the development of many digital texts that both engage digital rhetoric as method and object of analysis and as framework for the production of what we at the journal call "webtexts" (in order to differentiate them from "hypertexts," which hypertext theorists have claimed have somewhat different affordances and constraints than simply existing as texts on the Word Wide Web). Founded in 1996, *Kairos* has been the longest continually published online peer-reviewed academic journal in writing studies, and one of only a handful in the humanities in general that publish work that falls outside the genre of the traditional print scholarly article. Our goal has been to publish work that makes an academic argument not only through text but also through design, drawing on as many media and modes as an individual author cares to employ (see Ball [2004] and Ball & Moeller [2007] for arguments in favor of the value of this approach). In this section I'll review four webtexts published in *Kairos* between 2004 and 2011.

It was difficult to select just a few examples from among the very many available in *Kairos* (we have published well over three hundred webtexts in our first sixteen volumes), and, as senior editor of the journal, I certainly encourage readers of this work to peruse the current issue of *Kairos* and its archive, where you will find many more examples of digital-rhetoric-in-action. The four I have selected to review here all relate in some way to the theories presented in chapter 3, and each one deploys a variety of media types and interactions in order to represent their arguments. The webtexts I have selected are Ellen Cushman's (2004) "Composing New Media: Cultivating Landscapes of the Mind"; "Re-situating and Re-mediating the Canons: A Cultural-Historical Remapping of Rhetorical Activity" by Paul Prior, Janine Solberg, Patrick Berry, Hannah Bellwoar, Bill Chewning, Karen J. Lunsford, Liz Rohan, Kevin Roozen, Mary P. Sheridan-Rabideau, Jody Shipka, Derek Van Ittersum, and Joyce R. Walker (2007); Susan Delagrange's (2009) "*Wunderkammer*, Cornell, and the Visual Canon of Arrangement" (along with the follow-up *Inventio* article that describes the production process); and Justin Hodgson, Scott Nelson, Andrew Rechnitz, and Cleve Wiese's (2011) "The Importance of Undergraduate Multimedia: An Argument in Seven Acts."

The works we publish in *Kairos* should ideally invoke rhetoric as design as well as design as rhetorical practice; scholars should make their arguments not just verbally but also visually and structurally—in this sense, the aesthetic becomes rhetorical as well. As Cheryl Ball (2004) suggests in her discussion of new media scholarship, we need to "approach these texts with an appreciation of the aesthetic qualities that new media elements can offer toward creating the author's overall meaning" (413) when we read and critique these works; a reciprocal move should therefore be in play when producing this kind of scholarly work.

Because these are digital-native works, I will provide only a brief description of each (Cushman's work, in particular, requires interaction for the user to make meaning from the piece and a textual description will most definitely not be able to capture the essence or the argument of her webtext), focusing instead on why these are important examples of digital rhetoric practice.

"Composing New Media: Cultivating Landscapes of the Mind"

The crux of the argument in this work is presented through the requirement of interaction—in each screen, the user can move elements, click on them, or mouse-over to achieve different effects; the user is presented with a new screen of interactive possibility in response to the user's actions. There are no instructions, and no clear indications of what effect any given interaction may have on the current screen—the user is required to play with the interface in order to access enough of the overall design to begin to understand that the argument is about design choices and about both the constraints and affordances of interactivity itself. There is an explanatory essay that discusses the goals of the webtext and its overall argument, but it is inaccessible unless the user finds it in the course of interacting with the design. (This explanatory text was originally available at the outset of the webtext, but the editorial board members who served as peer-reviewers requested that it be made available as a result of the interaction, rather than as an alternative means to present the argument that would allow the user/reader to circumvent the requirement to play with the design.) This work is particularly interesting for the way that it portrays interactivity, and the way that it enacts its argument nonverbally, using only image and motion. Like Wysocki's (2002) "Bookling Monument," this is one of the *Kairos* webtexts that has completely erased the traditional elements of the genre of the academic essay.

"Re-situating and Re-mediating the Canons: A Cultural-Historical Remapping of Rhetorical Activity"

One of the reasons that I think this work is important is that it reimagines the canons of classical rhetoric through a cultural-historical activity theory lens and then provides examples of how such a revision would be enacted in the production of digital texts. It is digital rhetoric both in the sense of addressing the issue of reframing the canons in digital contexts and in the wide range of examples that accompany the core argument. This work is also one of many we have published that have far more authors than is common in humanities scholarship (twelve in this case). The authors provide a series of individually or jointly authored "data nodes" that are arranged around a central "core" argument. In the main argument, the authors contend "that a new set of canons is needed to re-situate rhetoric in complex sociohistoric worlds and to realize not simply a consistent multimodality, but a deep orientation to mediated activity and agency. Re-situating and re-mediating the canons takes us beyond any single setting and mode and offers a new map for an expansive attention to the rhetorical dimensions of all activity" (25). The data nodes around the core argument use different media and take up a range of different topics and ideas (they don't map neatly onto the elements of the main argument as examples so much as they *enact* some elements of those arguments—another of the key features of digital rhetoric scholarship).

"Wunderkammer, Cornell, and the Visual Canon of Arrangement"

In this webtext, Susan Delagrange presents a digital *wunderkammer* (a box of curios that held doors and drawers full of smaller objects) that the user opens in order to examine each of the elements of the overall argument. Much of the work focuses on arrangement in digital rhetoric, placing examples and instantiations of the argument alongside explanatory text found on each lexia. Delagrange introduces the webtext by explaining that her work with digital media

> focuses on the complementary areas of embodied digital representation and the canon of arrangement refigured as techné, as a productive art of arranging (bodies of) evidence to discover ethical bases for action. For me, designing constructive digital media is a process of mapping and remapping our physical and conceptual worlds in order to determine their meaning. (n.p.)

This approach to arrangement is carried out via mapping and remapping within the webtext itself.

I selected this piece in particular because we published a follow-up webtext in a new section we instituted in the journal called "Inventio." This new section aims to uncover and show the overall process that leads to the production of a webtext, providing access to the author's design decisions as well as editorial feedback and responses. In "When Revision is Redesign: Key Questions for Digital Scholarship," Delagrange (2009) helps to answer an important question for born-digital scholarly works:

When the interface of an interactive, digital, scholarly article is designed as an integral part of the article's argument, what are the rhetorical, conceptual, and technical challenges of re-designing the project to better enact that argument?

This kind of meta-reflection is critically important for producers of digital rhetoric scholarship, both to show that the process is indeed scholarly (and not simply aesthetic) and that the production of this kind of text is deeply labor-intensive, from both technical and intellectual perspectives.

"The Importance of Undergraduate Multimedia: An Argument in Seven Acts"

This webtext, built in Adobe Flash, utilizes text, audio, video, and animation in a series of seven vignettes, each of which draws on a different media metaphor: tower-configuration desktop PC, flash drive, Macintosh OS interface, super-8 projector, DJs turntables, comic book, and antique camera. Each piece reimagines the medium or platform—for instance, the PC becomes a three-dimensional model that becomes a museum of past technologies as the user zooms inside of it; the comic book has an animated computer screen in one panel, a short film in another. Each act has its own visual and auditory aesthetic (some of the acts were designed to be listened to using headphones, as there are two distinct audio channels). Although the overall argument is about the value of teaching multimedia production as part of the undergraduate curriculum in rhetoric/composition, the form that it takes also realizes several degrees of what Bolter and Grusin (1999) would consider remediation (although more on the side of hypermediation than of transparency). Each act also deftly uses juxtaposition and intertextuality as a rhetorical device. The framing device (and interface) for all of the acts is represented as a classical theatre, with red curtains and proscenium arch (yet another remediation of a more traditional or analog form). Each of the acts is persuasive in its own right (some taking more practical approaches to the value of teaching multimedia design and others focusing on the critical/theoretical rationales), but the sum of the acts leads to a well-developed and cohesive claim. In effect, acting as discrete units that function both together and separately, this work both enacts and champions digital rhetoric.

The examples I have selected here are several of the impressive scholarly works that both interrogate and enact digital rhetoric practices; but digital rhetoric is not a purely academic pursuit and the following section focuses on the development of new media forms for artistic and political purposes.

Digital Rhetoric and Production: Rhetoric, Design, Code

In this final series of examples, we'll look at digital rhetoric as employed in the production of a range of digital texts, including websites, remixes, multimodal composition, and games. I'll first review examples from three key texts in digital rhetoric—Warnick's *Rhetoric Online*, Bogost's *Persuasive Games*, and Losh's *Virtualpolitik*—and then provide three examples of digital rhetoric at work: DJ Kutiman's Thru-You project, Sean Tevis's political campaign for Kansas House of Representatives, and a selection of exemplary parodies and remixes.

Rhetoric at Work: Parodies, Government Sites, and Games

In her chapter on intertextuality and public discourse in *Rhetoric Online*, Warnick focuses mainly on two examples that use parody as a rhetorical trope in order to engage in political speech and media activism through digital rhetoric. The first example concerns animated parodies produced by jibjab.com, one that addresses the George W. Bush and John F. Kerry campaigns from the 2004 presidential election ("This Land is Your Land") and one that critiques the pharmaceutical industry ("The Drugs I Need").[1] Warnick situates the rhetorical appeal of these parodies in their use of intertextuality and reads the examples "in light of their relation to recognizable public events and themes, the verbal and visual texts the parodies draw on and the message they convey" in order to "illustrate how JibJab exploits its textual and contextual environments to hold users' attention and influence their thinking" (111). The second example in the chapter comes from Adbusters's use of parody in pursuit of media activism and culture jamming, focusing mainly on the use of spoof ads that are static, visual texts.

While the moves that Warnick makes point to some of the most prolific new media forms on the Internet (parodies, remixes, mashups) and provide a solid reading of their use of intertextuality as a rhetorical appeal, the methods are those of traditional rhetorical analysis, and the end result is that the examples don't appear to be any different than a printed visual parody or video parody despite their existence as digital texts.

In *Virtualpolitik*, Elizabeth Losh, like Warnick, is interested in political speech, but she is more concerned with the deployment of digital rhetoric as a means of power and control on the part of governments and bureaucracies than on public deliberation, activism, or resistance (although these moves do play a role in her project as well).

Like Warnick, Losh also addresses parody as a rhetorical construct, but rather than reading individual texts, she looks at the activities and processes that make such parody possible, from the affordances of replication in everyday software, to digital photo manipulation available in image editing programs, to online instances of "auto-generators" that create digital text representations of real-world objects in response to user input (such as the creation of fake airline boarding passes, warrants, or images of text on signs outside of churches). She charts the serious repercussions of the tension between parody-makers and government institutions and interrogates the way the digital rhetoricians who make the parodies are characterized: "While fans are seen as parasitic and lacking in content-creation abilities, hackers are seen as devious and likely to subvert the deliberative practices that others engage in openly and honestly. In other words, both groups are portrayed in print and broadcast culture as bad citizens who abuse existing power relationships" (200).

But Losh's examples of digital rhetoric as text and activity are not limited to parody, and she examines a wide range of genres, from the home pages of the websites of members of the US House of Representatives Intelligence Committee (21–24), to the extensive use of PowerPoint as a communicative medium by government agencies (165–81), to government-sponsored digital library initiatives (239–79). Losh also examines both military-funded videogames and simulations and serious games about national security and health as government-produced examples of digital rhetoric, much as Ian Bogost takes up videogames as sites of digital rhetoric in *Persuasive Games*.

In *Persuasive Games*, Bogost argues for a new digital rhetoric approach that he calls "procedural rhetoric" because the internal logic of processes within digital texts (and in nondigital texts as well, including workplaces, organizations, and institutions) supports the persuasive activities of those texts. Learning to read game-logic can lead to opportunities to work against the hard-coded paradigms and also to learn to expose how these processes work as agents of influence both in and out of games: "Videogames themselves cannot produce events; they are, after all, representations. But they can help members of a situation address the logic that guides it and begin to make movements to improve it" (332). Bogost examines a number of games, including the controversial *Grand Theft Auto: San Andreas*, "to show how the production of discourse can help trace the status of persuasion in procedural rhetorics" (333).

What is compelling about the examples used in each of these cases is the range of digital texts that are available for critique using digital rhetoric methods; but these examples also highlight the way that digital rhetoric undergirds the production of digital texts (whether implicitly or explicitly). The more sophisticated analytic methods employed by Losh and Bogost help to reveal not just the effect of these texts but the principles that drive their production. In the next sections, I will provide additional examples of digital rhetoric at work in the process of production for multimodal/multimedia composition (taking up Warnick's focus on parody, appropriation, and remix, and adding circulation as a rhetorical feature) and how rhetoric can be deployed not just through the surface features of digital texts but in the code itself.

Multimodal/Multimedia Composition: Appropriation, Remix, Circulation

In the tradition of digital rhetoric scholars that have come before me, I will present a series of examples that illustrate specific engagement with digital rhetoric practices or methods. Although the first series of examples is brief, I will finish with more in-depth considerations of multimedia composing and circulation as rhetorical practice. The following examples have in common a focus on remediation, appropriation, and remix as practices of rhetorical production.

Textual Appropriation and Remix

At spam-poetry.com (a no longer extant site), Kristin Thomas produced poetry from the subject lines of spam email, a practice she began in 2003. On her site, she noted that she saw her work as "a little bit Found Art, a little bit Whimsy, and mostly, just to find a way for me to find a peaceful intersection between digital communication and my life" (qtd. in Hurvitz, 2006). Although likely not the first person to create poetry from spam, Thomas's work received a great deal of attention and inspired others to create their own spam poetry (or "spoetry"). The genre of spam poetry has become quite popular, and a number of fine examples can be found on the website of the Spam Poetry Institute (http://www.spampoetry.org), which bills itself as "an organization dedicated to collecting and preserving the fine literature created by the world's spammers."

Jonathan Lethem, author of *You Don't Love Me Yet*, is offering several stories on his website (http://jonathanlethem.com/promiscuous_materials.html) for others to appropriate, remix, and adapt (but not copy in their entirety). On his site, he explains that he likes "art that comes from other art" and likes to see his stories adapted into other forms: "My writing has always been strongly sourced in other voices, and I'm a fan of adaptations, appropriations, collage, and sampling."

Micah Ian Wright's "Propaganda Remix Project" (http://propagandaremix.com) presents classic wartime propaganda posters with new, antiwar slogans replacing the originals. In this case, the remix happens at the littoral zone of contact between text and image.

A blogger who goes by the handle "Canis Lupus" has created a parody re-mix (http://www.aaronsw.com/2002/valentiRemix) of Jack Valenti's "Moral Imperative" speech, given at Duke University February 24, 2003; this remix converts Valenti's antipiracy message into a pro-fair-use rights message.

Peter Gabriel has created a site that promotes the remixing of his and other artists' work; at Real World Remixed (http://realworldrecords.com/remixed), users are encouraged to "to download our 'sample packs'—multitrack re-cordings from Real World Records and Peter Gabriel" and use them to cre-ate remixes, which are then uploaded to the site and voted upon by other site users. (See, for example, http://realworldrecords.com/remixed/group/84776/peter-gabriel-shock-the-monkey-remix-competition.)

An anonymous artist has created a mashup of rapper 50 cent's "In Da Club" and "Yakkety Sax" (better known as the theme song from the Benny Hill show); this is considered a mashup rather than a remix because neither song was edited for content, they were simply layered one atop the other (although the 50 cent song was sped up just a bit). The mashup, accompanied by the original video for "In Da Club," is available on YouTube (http://youtube.com/watch?v=jkyc1dxL3N0).

In 2006, Luis Hernandez and Paul Holcomb (http://www.boldheaded.com/podcast) created a techno-dance track that featured an edited and re-mixed version of former Alaska senator Ted Stevens's commentary on net neutrality (they later created an even more pointed parody remix using more of Stevens's words to create another techno-dance song called "The Internet Must Die").

Appropriation and Editing (Remix)

Working in both audio and (music) video, Alanis Morissette has produced a parody video of the Black Eyed Peas song "My Humps." Although she does not change the lyrics, her ballad-like rendition certainly provides pointed com-mentary on those lyrics, and the video itself has many elements of the original video for the song, thus qualifying as remix. This example is also available on YouTube (http://youtu.be/pRmYfVCH2UA); however, there doesn't appear to be an official upload, so it is likely that NBC Universal will at some point issue a takedown notice for copyright infringement.

Johan Söderberg created a parody that synchronizes several different video clips of George W. Bush and Tony Blair in a way that appears to show them singing Diana Ross and Lionel Richie's "Endless Love" to each other (http://politicalhumor.about.com/od/bushvideos/youtube/bushblairlove.htm)

A popular form of video remix for anime fans is the creation of music vid-eos: clips from anime cartoon serials or films are edited together to create a video that thematically represents (or even lip-synchs to) whatever song the remix producer has chosen.

One of the most impressive examples of multimodal composition, appropriation, and remix that I have seen thus far is the "Thru-You" project created by an Israeli DJ who goes by Kutiman (http://thru-you.com). Kutiman selected clips from several hundred video posts to YouTube, mostly of people playing instruments or singing (some include instructional videos, others are children showing off their musical skills, and one memorable example is of a mother singing a lullaby to her baby); Kutiman extracted the audio from these clips and remixed them into an album's worth of original songs—these video clips became the instrument he played as he crafted his composition (http://www.youtube.com/watch?v=tprMEs-zfQA).

But Kutiman didn't just use the music; he cut all of the video together in technically precise configurations to create a visual representation for each of the songs as well. He also provided a means to access a series of citations that can be followed back to the original clips, and placed the full project on a website that collects all of these multimodal compositions together so they are available and accessible through a single interface—an interface that appropriates and remixes the interface of YouTube itself (http://www.youtube.com/watch?v=KzogYbqOZXQ).

This is a masterful example of arrangement as invention and of the ways in which digital networks can provide the means to discover new forms and new ways of making meaning via the (re)combination and juxtaposition of digital texts.

Rhetoric *in* the Code

As a final example, I want to relate a case that enacts digital rhetoric in a number of ways: Sean Tevis for Kansas State Representative. Tevis's campaign first gained national recognition for a cartoon that he drew to explain why he was running. The cartoon was an appropriation (and, in part, homage) to XKCD, a very popular comic among those who consider themselves Internet savvy (the comic is subtitled "A Webcomic of Romance, Sarcasm, Math, and Language"). In addition, the comic referenced a number of Internet-specific activities (such as "downmodding" or adding negative votes against an online comment) and rick-rolling; Tevis also drew on the then-popular meme of creating parodies of the film 300 (itself a remediation of Frank Miller's graphic novel). Tevis's comic was so well executed that it was noticed by the same audience who reads XKCD and was circulated through a number of blogs and news aggregator sites (such as metafilter.com and fark.com). Once the link to his site was in greater circulation, more and more people went to view it and pass on the link, to the point where he received enough exposure to be noticed by the mainstream media, which garnered him a number of television and print news interviews.

One of the reasons that such circulation qualifies as digital rhetoric as productive force is that Tevis's appeal was an intentional bid to reach a wider audience (and it is likely that he had a specific kind of audience in mind: one that would agree with his progressive policy stance): "I made an appeal that was both personal and that leveraged the power of social networks to quickly communicate with others. . . . By using the ability to collaborate online, connect with an audience, and communicate in a way that, say, mailing a brochure simply can't, we were able to break the record for the most number of donors to a State Representative campaign in Kansas."

Tevis did not just have a comic, however, he had a website for his campaign—a website that included an option to donate to the campaign via Pay-Pal. The stated goal expressed in the comic was to convince three thousand people to each donate $8.34 (which he had calculated would yield the minimum amount—$26,000—to run a potentially successful campaign). In less than forty-eight hours, he had reached his goal; over the span of two months he received over $100,000.

Although Tevis's use of the comic format, intertextual references, and knowledge of how to leverage aggregators and blogs for circulation (the latter being an example of what Jim Ridolfo [2005] would call "rhetorical velocity") would qualify as an example of digital rhetoric, I was also interested in the way that he developed his ethos via a hidden appeal designed to communicate with a technologically knowledgeable audience. On the page of the campaign website that included the comic, the following was placed in a comment in the HTML source code: "Hello person who cares enough to read source code. Please donate $8.88 to my campaign. Any amount with 88 cents at the end is flagged for me to let me know that it came from someone who I guess is a lot like me. You'll also be entered into a drawing to win a prize and it will help save the world. Thank you." In other words, Tevis used all of the persuasive resources at his disposal to increase the success of his argument that there was value in supporting his candidacy.

While the comic and website proved to be financially successful, Tevis ultimately lost the election (although it was fairly close at 52–48 percent, which is a positive outcome for a young, first-time candidate running against a three-term incumbent). In fact, the fundraising tactic was perhaps too successful, as after the election a bill was introduced that would require full disclosure of contributors who donated even small amounts to a campaign, but only if those small donations reached over $1000 (in other words, it added an onerous accounting requirement that would only kick in for situations like the one that Tevis engineered). Nonetheless, the employment of digital rhetoric practices propelled the campaign to much greater visibility and success than would otherwise have been possible with more traditional campaign marketing techniques.

Digital Rhetoric Practice—Call for Case Studies

One of the difficulties of working with digital rhetoric—and particularly with publishing works on the moving targets of digital innovation and online activity—is that many of these examples have moved or vanished just in the six months between my original draft of the chapter and a subsequent revision. It is therefore important for digital rhetoric scholars to archive the digital products they study. It is equally important that born-digital scholarly work consider issues of stability and sustainability and select appropriate venues for publication. I plan to review and update the links to examples in the digital version of this text on a quarterly basis, which should help to keep the links current. But there are, of course, many other examples of digital rhetoric practice currently available for examination and research, not to mention new forms (such as mobile applications, augmented reality systems, and digital games) that I have not covered here. Thus I end this chapter with a call for digital rhetoric case studies and continued work on areas covered in this book. There are three venues in particular that I would recommend to digital rhetoric scholars:

The Sweetland Digital Rhetoric Collaborative (http://www.digitalrhetoric collaborative.org/about), which hosts a curated blog, a digital rhetoric wiki, and a new digital rhetoric book series published by the University of Michigan Press.

H-DigiRhet (http://www.h-net.org/~digirhet/) is a discussion list (part of the H-Net collective of discussion and reviews-oriented lists). The H-DigiRhet network provides an online discussion space for teachers, researchers, and scholars who are working at the intersections of writing, rhetoric, communication, and digital technologies, focusing on issues of digital composition, computer-mediated communication (CMC), digital literacy, information and communication technologies (ICTs), human-computer interaction (HCI), and digital rhetoric. The list has over six hundred subscribers as of June 2012, and it is a perfect venue for announcing digital rhetoric work to an interested audience; the list and reviews editors also seek reviews of books and digital projects related to digital rhetoric.

And, of course, as senior editor of *Kairos: A Journal of Rhetoric, Technology, and Pedagogy* (http://kairos.technorhetoric.net), I welcome born-digital submissions (that we call "webtexts") that take up questions of digital rhetoric theory, method, or practice.

Coda

I hope that this book will serve as a useful resource to students and scholars and will provide a framework for digital rhetoric scholarship, as well as a representation of the scope and interests of digital rhetoric as an emerging field of study. I also hope to see a surge in works that address digital rhetoric across several fields of inquiry, and I welcome your updates, suggestions, and queries.

Notes

Introduction

1. Lev Manovich begins *The Language of New Media* with his own personal chronology, which situates his disciplinary perspective within the field of digital art—and it is in part the differences in these disciplinary origins that distinguish digital rhetoric and new media. For a similar technology literacy narrative in the field of computers and writing, see James Porter's (2002) "A Cyberwriter's Tale."

2. A more detailed account of my academic history may be found in Eyman, D. (2005). Moving in from the periphery: Exploring the disciplinary labyrinth. In James Inman & Beth Hewett (Eds.), *Technology and English studies: Innovative professional paths* (75–89). Mahwah, NJ: Lawrence Erlbaum.

3. Because the system was only marketed (and not produced) by Timex, we had to ship the inert computer to England so it could be repaired by the Sinclair technicians, and my actual use of the machine did not commence until the following year. This may in part also explain why I've never been as interested in the hardware elements of computing systems.

4. In the particular instance that comes to mind, I was using Usenet newsgroups and a moo in my first-year writing course and had to find a way to connect the server in my office to the computers in the classroom—because connection to the Internet was not allowed, I had to establish local instances of these platforms.

5. The MOO is an object-oriented variant of the Multi-User Domain (MUD), a text-based, editable, online, multiuser system that supported both synchronous chat and the building of rooms, objects, and bots that would always be available to users. Early versions of MUDs were similar to text-based role-playing games (like *Colossal Cave Adventure* and ZORK) and were designed to facilitate multiuser role playing (by some accounts, the "D" in MUD originally stood for "Dungeon"). For more on the history and uses of MUDs and MOOs, see Holmevik & Haynes (1999); many of the participants in the Tuesday night discussions published about using MOOs for teaching writing in the *Kairos* 1.2 CoverWeb, "Pedagogies in Virtual Spaces: Writing Classes in the MOO" (http://kairos.technorhetoric.net/1.2). For an overview and representation of the Tuesday Café discussions, see in particular Sharon Cogdill's (1996) contribution, "@go tuesday."

6. For more detailed histories and uses of the term, see Day (2009).

7. This is James Berlin's term (roughly synonymous with social-epistemic rhetoric) for rhetorical practices that acknowledge and engage the social construction of knowledge. See Berlin, James. (1988). Rhetoric and ideology in the writing class. *College English*, 50(5): 477–94.

8. I had met many computers and writing scholars (whom I now count as friends

and colleagues) the previous year at the Conference on College Composition and Communication, but the Computers and Writing Conference is where the most cutting-edge, interdisciplinary work is presented; it is also a much smaller conference that is widely known to be very welcoming to newcomers.

9. For more on the history of the field as represented through its main conference, see Gerrard, Lisa. (1995). The evolution of the Computers and Writing Conference. *Computers and Composition*, 12(3): 279–92, and the follow-up in Gerrard, Lisa. (2006). The evolution of the Computers and Writing Conference: The second decade. *Computers and Composition*, 23(2): 211–27.

10. For details on the history of the journal, see Doherty (2001) and Salvo & Doherty (2002).

11. To learn more about *Kairos* and its history, see Bridgeford (2006), Kalmbach (2006), and Eyman (2006)—all from the tenth anniversary issue.

Chapter 1

1. I subscribe to the position that rhetoric is, indeed, foundational and implicit in all communication; to be sure, however, this position is contested and has been subject to interpretation over the long history of rhetoric itself.

2. On "memory," see, for instance, Gossett (2008), Hess (2007), and Haskins (2007); on "delivery," see Ridolfo (2005) and Porter (2009 and 2010).

3. See Horak (2007) for a technical discussion of the differences between analog and digital signals.

4. This quality of intertextuality echoes Bakhtin's notion of the "utterance," which he defines as a thought which is given voice (either in speech or in writing) (1981, p. 272); as Michael Holquist (1990) argues, every "utterance is always an answer to another utterance that precedes it, and is therefore always conditioned by, and in turn qualifies, the prior utterance to a greater or lesser degree" (60). Latour (1988) takes this idea one step further and argues that a text is shaped both by predecessors and by those texts that come after (and refer to) it. Clearly, intertextuality invokes both a network of relationships and temporal situatedness, both of which have implications for digital rhetoric.

5. Kress focuses on the mode of writing specifically, but I argue that texts, which can be multimodal or built from multimedia resources, should not be limited to a single mode (much less "writing," which evokes the notion of text-as-printed-word that I am trying to move away from in our understanding of "text").

6. She notes that communication departments typically categorize themselves as social science rather than humanities and are thus not implicated in this critique (Welch, 1999, p. 5, note 1).

7. Zappen's article in fact serves as a kind of model for my approach to defining and locating "digital rhetoric" here in chapter 1.

8. See Toulmin's (1969) *The Uses of Argument*.

9. Perhaps part of the problem is that rhetorical theorists such as Foucault, Derrida, Barthes, etc. are often considered part of literary theory because their work has been extensively applied to the study of literary texts; however, given the purview of rhetoric, it is a mistake to limit these theorists to the relatively new branch of rhetoric that deals with the study of literary texts.

10. In this case and in the following examples she uses "genre" in the taxonomic

sense rather than the term developed and expanded upon by rhetorical genre studies.

11. Losh is here drawing on Lanham's (1993) "The implications of electronic information for the sociality of knowledge" available at http://www.cni.org/docs/tsh/Lanham.html.

12. See, for instance, the section on cybermetrics in chapter 3, "Digital Rhetoric: Method."

13. Work in artificial intelligence (AI) research shows that AI researchers certainly think this is the case—see, for instance, Reed & Norman (2004) and Lopes, Wooldridge, & Novais (2008).

14. See the introduction for a more detailed history of the term "technorhetorician."

15. Ulmer's more recent work in *Internet Invention* (2003) is covered in chapter 3.

16. Manovich's own dismissal of rhetoric, which I believe is based on a fundamental misunderstanding of what rhetoric is and does, will not prevent me for claiming this method as rhetorical, especially in its examples of cultural logics and ideological affects.

17. It is possible that the ill-advised approach to developing a mathematical topology for digital rhetoric is in part influenced by Manovich's first principle.

18. HASTAC is the Humanities, Arts, Science, and Technology Advanced Collaboratory—"HASTAC ('haystack') is a network of individuals and institutions inspired by the possibilities that new technologies offer us for shaping how we learn, teach, communicate, create, and organize our local and global communities" (from http://hastac.org/about).

19. For more on the establishment of the modern English department and the relationship of rhetoric and literary study, see Susan Miller (1991).

Chapter 2

1. To be fair, Lanham does eventually make a stronger connection between style and substance, noting that if you "push style to its extreme and it becomes substance" (255)—but this still maintains style and substance as distinct entities (albeit collaborative ones rather than oppositional). And the previous two hundred and fifty pages prior to this admission have maintained that distinction.

2. In 1866, zoologist Enrst Haeckel coined the term "ecology" to define an area of biology that aimed to study the interrelationships between organisms and the environment (Bramwell, 1989).

Chapter 4

1. Curiously, Warnick states that JibJab's use of its website and web content was "not limited to political parody," which she sets up in opposition to the pharmaceutical industry critique (111). Warnick appears to be using a very restricted definition of "political"—much like the very limited approach she takes to "rhetoric."

References

Adler, Stephen. (1998). Preserving the information ecosystem. *FreshMeat.* http://fresh-meat.net/articles/view/124.

Aguillo, Isidro F. (2003). Cybermetrics: Definitions and methods for an emerging discipline. Lecture presented for the European Indicators, Cyberspace and the Science-Technology-Economy System. http://www.eicstes.org/EICSTES_PDF/PRESENTATIONS/Cybermetrics%20(Aguillo).PDF.

Aristotle. (1991). *On rhetoric: A theory of civic discourse.* Trans. George Kennedy. New York: Oxford University Press.

Arnold, Carroll. (1982). Introduction. In Chaim Perelman, *The Realm of Rhetoric* (vii–xx). Notre Dame, IN: University of Notre Dame Press.

Arroyo, Sarah. (2009). Seminar in Digital Rhetoric. (Course Syllabus). Long Beach: California State Universty. http://www.csulb.edu/~dtsuyuki/saraharroyo/cv-pdfs/DigitalRhetoricSpring09–1.pdf.

Aune, James Arnt. (1997). The work of rhetoric in the age of digital dissemination. *Quarterly Journal of Speech,* 83(2): 230–42.

Bakhtin, M. M. (1981). Discourse in the novel. In M. Holquist (Ed.), *The dialogic imagination: Four essays by M. M. Bakhtin.* (C. Emerson & M. Holquist, Trans.). Austin: University of Texas Press.

Ball, Cheryl E. (2004). Show, not tell: The value of new media scholarship. *Computers and Composition,* 21(4): 403–25.

Ball, Cheryl E., & Moeller, Ryan M. (2007). Reinventing the possibilities: Academic literacy and new media. *Fibreculture Journal,* 10: http://journal.fibreculture.org/issue10/ball_moeller/index.html.

Ballif, Michelle. (1998). Writing the third-sophistic cyborg: periphrasis on an [in]tense rhetoric. *Rhetoric Society Quarterly,* 28(4): 51–67.

Barilli, Renato. (1989). *Rhetoric.* Trans. Giuliana Minozzi. Minneapolis: University of Minnesota Press.

Barnes, Joseph A. (1954). Class and committees in a Norwegian island parish. *Human Relations,* 7: 39–58.

Barnes, Joseph A. (1972). *Social networks.* Reading, MA: Addison-Wesley.

Barrett, Edward (Ed.). (1988). *Text, context, and hypertext: Writing with and for the computer.* Cambridge, MA: MIT Press.

Barthes, Roland. (1974). *S/Z.* Trans. Richard Miller. New York: Noonday.

Barthes, Roland. (1977). *Image-Music-Text.* Trans. Stephen Heath. London: Fontana.

Basgier, Christopher. (2011). The author-function, the genre function, and the rhetoric of scholarly webtexts. *Computers and Composition,* 28(2): 145–59.

Bay, Jennifer. (2010). Body on >body<: Coding subjectivity. In Bradley Dilger and

Jeff Rice (Eds.), *From A to <A>: Keywords in markup* (150–66). Minneapolis: University of Minnesota Press.

Bayer, Alan E., Smart, John C., & McLaughlin, Gerald W. (1990). Mapping intellectual structure of a scientific subfield through author cocitations. *Journal of the American Society for Information Science*, 41(6): 444–52.

Bazerman, Charles. (1999). *The languages of Edison's light*. Cambridge, MA: MIT Press.

Bazerman, Charles (Ed.). (2007). *Handbook of research on writing: History, society, school, individual, text*. New York: Routledge.

Berkenkotter, Carol, & Huckin, Thomas. (1995). *Genre knowledge in disciplinary communication: Cognition/culture/power*. Mahwah, NJ: Lawrence Erlbaum.

Berlin, James. (1988). Rhetoric and ideology in the writing class. *College English*, 50(5): 477–94.

Biesecker, Barbara. (1999). Rethinking the rhetorical situation from within the thematic of différance. In John Lucatites, Celeste Condit, & Sally Caudill (Eds.), *Contemporary Rhetorical Theory* (232–46). New York: The Guilford Press.

Bitzer, Lloyd. (1968). The rhetorical situation. *Philosophy and Rhetoric*, 1: 1–14.

Bizzell, Patricia, & Herzberg, Bruce. (2000). *The rhetorical tradition: Readings from classical times to the present* (2nd ed.). Boston: Bedford/St. Martin's.

Black, Edwin. (1965). *Rhetorical criticism: A study in method*. Madison: University of Wisconsin Press.

Blakesley, David, & Brooke, Collin. (2001). Introduction: Notes on visual rhetoric. *Enculturation*, 3(2): http://enculturation.net/3_2/introduction.html.

Blakesley, David, & Rickert, Thomas. (2004). From nodes to nets: Our emerging culture of complex interactive networks. *JAC*, 24(4): 821–30.

Blythe, Stuart. (2007). Agencies, ecologies, and the mundane artifacts in our midst. In Pamela Takayoshi & Pat Sullivan (Eds.), *Labor, writing technologies, and the shaping of composition in the academy* (167–86). New York: Hampton Press.

Bobley, Brett. (2008). Why the digital humanities? NEH Office of Digital Humanities. http://www.neh.gov/whoweare/cio/odhfiles/Why.The.Digital.Humanities.pdf.

Bogost, Ian. (2007). *Persuasive games*. Cambridge, MA: MIT Press.

Bogost, Ian, & Monfort, Nick. (2006). Platform studies. http://platformstudies.com.

Bolter, Jay David. (1991). *Writing space: The computer, hypertext, and the history of writing*. Hillsdale, NJ: Lawrence Erlbaum.

Bolter, Jay David, & Grusin, Richard. (1999). *Remediation: Understanding new media*. Cambridge, MA: MIT Press.

Bourdieu, Pierre. (1993). *The Field of Cultural Production*. Ed. Randal Johnson. New York: Columbia University Press.

Bourdieu, Pierre. (1986). The forms of capital. Trans. Richard Nice. In John G. Richardson (Ed.), *Handbook of theory and research for the sociology of education* (241–58). New York: Greenwood Press.

Bourdieu, Pierre. (1988). *Homo Academicus*. Trans. Peter Collier. Palo Alto, CA: Stanford University Press.

Bourdieu, Pierre. (1977). *Outline of a theory of practice*. Trans. Richard Nice. Cambridge, UK: Cambridge University Press.

Bourdieu, Pierre, & Wacquant, Loïc. (1992). *An invitation to reflexive sociology*. Chicago: University of Chicago Press.

Bowker, Geoffrey, & Star, Susan Leigh. (1996). How things (actor-net)work: Classification, magic and the ubiquity of standards. http://www.sis.pitt.edu/~gbowker/actnet.html.

Bramwell, Anna. (1989). *Ecology in the 20th century: A history.* New Haven, CT: Yale University Press.

Brent, Doug. (1997). Rhetorics of the web: Implications for teachers of literacy. *Kairos: A Journal of Rhetoric, Technology, and Pedagogy,* 2(1): http://kairos.technorhetoric.net/2.1/features/brent/bridge.html.

Brewer, Richard. (1988). *The science of ecology.* New York: Saunders College Publishing.

Bridgeford, Tracy. (2006). Kairotically speaking: Kairos and the power of identity. *Kairos: A Journal of Rhetoric, Technology, and Pedagogy,* 11(1): http://kairos.technorhetoric.net/11.1/binder.html?topoi/bridgeford/index.htm.

Brock, Kevin. (2010). Open source software and the construction of electronic identities. Presented at the Carolina Rhetoric Conference, Raleigh, NC.

Broder, Andrei et al. (2000). Graph structure in the Web. *Journal of Computer Networks,* 33(1–6): 309–20.

Brooke, Collin G. (2009). *Lingua fracta: Toward a rhetoric of new media.* Cresskill, NJ: Hampton Press.

Brooke, Collin G. (2011). To affinity . . . and beyond! Rhetoric from a network perspective. Paper presented at the Center for Writing Studies colloquium series, University of Illinois at Urbana-Champaign.

Brown, Roger. (1965). *Social Psychology.* New York: Free Press.

Brummett, Barry. (2010). *Techniques of close reading.* Thousand Oaks, CA: Sage.

Buchanan, Richard. (1989). Declaration by design: Rhetoric, argument, and demonstration in design practice. In Victor Margolin (Ed.), *Design discourse: History, theory, criticism* (91–109). Chicago: University of Chicago Press.

Budd, John M. (1999). Citations and knowledge claims: Sociology of knowledge as a case in point. *Journal of Information Science,* 25(4): 265–74.

Bunge, Mario. (1979). A systems concept of society: Beyond individualism and holism. *Theory and Decision,* 10(1): 13–30.

Burbules, Nicholas C. (1998). Rhetorics of the web: Hyperreading and critical literacy. In Ilana Snyder (Ed.), *Page to screen: taking literacy into the electronic era* (102–22). London: Routledge.

Burke, Kenneth J. (1966). *Language as symbolic action: Essays on life, literature, and method.* Berkley: University of California Press.

Burke, Kenneth J. (1969). *A rhetoric of motives.* Berkeley: University of California Press.

Burton, Gideon. (2004). *Silva Rhetoricae.* http://humanities.byu.edu/rhetoric/Canons/Style.htm.

Busch, Carol et al. (2005). Content analysis. Writing@CSU. Colorado State University Department of English. http://writing.colostate.edu/guides/research/content.

Callon, Michel. (1987). Society in the making: The study of technology as a tool for sociological analysis. In Wiebe E. Bijker, Thomas Parke Hughes, & Trevor J. Pinch (Eds.), *The social construction of technological systems: New directions in the sociology and history of technology (83–103).* Cambridge, MA: MIT Press.

Card, Stuart. (1993). Foreword. In Alan Dix et al., *Human-computer interaction* (xi–xii). New York: Prentice Hall.

Carlson, Patricia. (1990). The rhetoric of hypertext. *Hypermedia,* 2(2): 109–31.

Carnegie, Teena A. M. (2009). Interface as exordium: The rhetoric of interactivty. *Computers and Composition,* 26(2): 164–73.

Cicero. (1942). *De oratore.* Trans. E. W. Sutton & H. Rackham. Cambridge, MA: Harvard University Press.

Codgill, Sharon. (1996). @go tuesday. *Kairos: A Journal of Rhetoric, Technology, and Peda-*

gogy, 1(2): http://kairos.technorhetoric.net/1.2/binder2.html?coverweb/Cogdill/gotuesday.html.

Cohen, Michael E. (2002). Stalking the digital rhetoric. http://homepage.mac.com/lymond/digirhet.html.

Connors, Robert J. (1999). The rhetoric of citation systems, part 2: Competing epistemic values in citation. *Rhetoric Review*, 17(2): 219–45.

Consigny, Scott. (1974). Rhetoric and its situations. *Philosophy and Rhetoric*, 7: 175–86.

Cooper, Marilyn M. (1986). The ecology of writing. *College English*, 46(4): 364–75.

Coover, Robert. (1999). Literary hypertext: The passing of the golden age. Keynote address at the Digital Arts and Culture Conference, Atlanta, GA. http://nickm.com/vox/golden_age.html.

Corby, Katherine. (2001). Method or madness? Educational research and citation prestige. *Portal: Libraries and the academy*, 1(3): 279–88.

Covino, William. (1994). *Magic, rhetoric, and literacy*. New York: SUNY Press.

Cozzens, Susan E. (1989). What do citations count? The rhetoric first model. *Scientometrics*, 15: 437–47.

Cripps, Michael J. (2004). #FFFFFF,#000000, & #808080: Hypertext theory and webdev in the composition classroom. *Computers and Composition Online*: http://www.bgsu.edu/cconline/cripps/index.html.

Crosswhite, Jim et al. (2004). Computational models of rhetorical argument. In Chris Reed & Timothy Norman (Eds.), *Argumentation machines: New frontiers in argumentation and computation* (175–210). Dordrecht, The Netherlands: Kluwer Academic Publishers.

Cushman, Ellen. (2004). Composing new media: Cultivating landscapes of the mind. *Kairos: A Journal of Rhetoric, Technology, and Pedagogy*, 9(1): http://kairos.technorhetoric.net/9.1/binder.html?http://www.msu.edu/%7Ecushmane/one/landscape.html.

Darwish, Ali. (2008). *Optimality in translation*. Victoria, Canada: Writescope.

Davis, Robert L., & Shadle, Mark F. (2007). *Teaching multiwriting: Researching and composing with multiple genres, media, disciplines, and cultures*. Carbondale: Southern Illinois University Press.

Day, Michael. (2009). The administrator as technorhetorician: Sustainable technological ecologies in writing programs. In Dànielle Nicole DeVoss, Heidi A. McKee, & Richard Selfe (Eds.), *Technological ecologies and sustainability* (130–48). Computers and Composition Digital Press. http://ccdigitalpress.org/tes.

De Beaugrande, Robert, & Dressler, Wolfgang. (1981). *Introduction to text linguistics*. New York: Longman.

Delagrange, Susan H. (2009). When revision is redesign: Key questions for digital scholarship. *Kairos: A Journal of Rhetoric, Technology, and Pedagogy*, 14(1): http://kairos.technorhetoric.net/14.1/inventio/delagrange/index.html.

Delagrange, Susan H. (2009). Wunderkammer, Cornell, and the visual canon of arrangement. *Kairos: A Journal of Rhetoric, Technology, and Pedagogy*, 13(2): http://kairos.technorhetoric.net/13.2/topoi/delagrange/index.html.

DePew, Kevin. (2007). Through the eyes of researchers, rhetors, and audiences: Triangulating data from the digital writing situation. In Heidi McKee & Dànielle DeVoss (Eds.), *Digital Writing Research* (71–88). Cresskill, NJ: Hampton Press.

DeVoss, Dànielle Nicole, & Porter, James E. (2006). Why Napster matters to writing: Filesharing as a new ethic of digital delivery. *Computers and Composition*, 23(1): 178–210.

Diamandaki, Katerina. (2003). Virtual ethnicity and digital diasporas: Identity construction in cyberspace. *Global Media Journal*, 2(2): http://lass.calumet.purdue.edu/cca/gmj/sp03/graduatesp03/gmj-sp03grad-diamandaki.htm.

DigiRhet.org. (2006). Teaching digital rhetoric: Community, critical engagement, and application. *Pedagogy: Critical Approaches to Teaching Literature, Language, Composition, and Culture*, 6(20): 231–59.

DigiRhet.org. (2008). Old+old+old=new: A copyright manifesto for the digital world. *Kairos: A Journal of Rhetoric, Technology, and Pedagogy*, 12(3): http://kairos.technorhetoric.net/12.3/topoi/digirhet.

Dilger, Bradley. (2010). Beyond star flashes: The elements of Web 2.0 style. *Computers and Composition*, 27(1): 15–26.

Dix, Alan et al. (1993). *Human-computer interaction*. New York: Prentice Hall.

Doctorow, Cory. (2005). Bruce Sterling's design future manifesto: viva spime! *BoingBoing*: http://boingboing.net/2005/10/26/bruce-sterlings-desi.html.

Doherty, Mick. (2001). @Title this_chapter as . . . . [Was: On the web, nobody knows you're an editor]. In John F. Barber & Dene Grigar (Eds.), *New worlds, new words: Exploring pathways for writing about and in electronic environments* (95–120). Cresskill, NJ: Hampton.

Dorwick, Keith. (2005). From darkness to light: Struggling with the tenure-track. In James Inman & Beth Hewett (Eds.), *Technology and English studies: Innovative professional paths* (90–104). Mahwah, NJ: Lawrence Erlbaum.

Edbauer, Jenny. (2005). Unframing models of public distribution: From rhetorical situation to rhetorical ecologies. *Rhetoric Society Quarterly*, 35(4): 5–24.

English, James F. (2005). *The economy of prestige: Prizes, awards, and the circulation of cultural value*. Cambridge, MA: Harvard University Press.

Eyman, Douglas. (2005). Moving in from the periphery: Exploring the disciplinary labyrinth. In James Inman & Beth Hewett (Eds.), *Technology and English studies: Innovative professional paths* (75–89). Mahwah, NJ: Lawrence Erlbaum.

Eyman, Douglas. (2006). The arrow and the loom: A decade of *Kairos*. *Kairos: Rhetoric, Technology, Pedagogy*, 11(1): http://kairos.technorhetoric.net/11.1/binder.html?topoi/eyman/index.html.

Eyman, Douglas. (2009). Usability: Methodology and design practice for writing processes and pedagogies. In Susan Miller-Cochran & Rochelle Rodgrigo (Eds.), *Rhetorically rethinking usability* (213–28). Cresskill, NJ: Hampton Press.

Eyman, Douglas. (2011). Web Authoring and Design. (Course Syllabus). George Mason University. http://pwr.gmu.edu/course/342.

Eysenbach, Gunther. (2006). Citation advantage of open access journals. *PLoS Biology*, 4(5): e157. doi: 10.1371/journal.pbio.0040157.

Fagerjord, Anders. (2003). Rhetorical convergence: Studying web media. In Gunnar Liestøl, Andrew Morrison, and Terje Rasmussen (Eds.), *Digital media revisited: Theoretical and conceptual innovation in digital domains* (293–325). Cambridge, MA: MIT Press.

Faigley, Lester. (1998). Visual rhetoric: Literacy by design. Center for Interdisciplinary Studies of Writing Conference "Technology and Literacy in a Wired Academy." University of Minnesota, Minneapolis, MN.

Farkas, David, & Farkas, Jean. (2002). *Principles of web design*. New York: Longman.

Feenberg, Andrew. (1999). *Questioning technology*. New York: Routledge.

Foss, Sonja. (2004). Framing the study of visual rhetoric: Toward a transformation of rhetorical theory. In Charles Hill & Marguerite Helmers (Eds.), *Defining visual rhetorics* (303–13). Mahwah, NJ: Lawrence Erlbaum.

Foucault, Michel. (1972). *The archaeology of knowledge and the discourse on language.* Trans. A. M. Sheridan Smith. New York: Pantheon Books.

Fountain, Jane. (2001). *Building the virtual state: Information technology and institutional change.* Washington, DC: Brookings Institution.

Freeman, Kathleen. (1966). *The pre-Socratic philosophers: A companion to Diels Fragments der Voraskratiker.* (2nd ed.). Oxford, UK: Blackwell.

Freeman, Lin. (1997). What is network analysis?: The study of social networks. International Network for Social Network Analysis. http://web.archive.org/web/19970511163336/http://www.heinz.cmu.edu/project/INSNA/na_inf.html.

Galloway, Alexander. (2004). *Protocol: How control exists after decentralization.* Cambridge, MA: MIT Press.

Galloway, Alexander, & Thacker, Eugene. (2007). *The exploit: A theory of networks.* Minneapolis: University of Minnesota Press.

Garrett, Jesse James. (2011). *The elements of user experience: User-centered design for the web and beyond.* (2nd ed.). Berkeley, CA: New Riders.

Garson, G. David. (2006). *Public information technology and e-governance: Managing the virtual state.* Sudbury, MA: Jones and Bartlett.

Garton, L., Haythornthwaite, C., & Wellman, B. (1997). Studying online social networks. *Journal of Computer Mediated Communication,* 3(1): http://jcmc.indiana.edu/vol3/issue1/garton.html.

Gaydecki, Patrick. (2004). *Foundations of digital signal processing: Theory, algorithms, and hardware design.* London: The Institution of Electrical Engineers.

Gerrard, Lisa. (1995). The evolution of the Computers and Writing Conference. *Computers and Composition,* 12(3): 279–92.

Gerrard, Lisa. (2006). The evolution of the Computers and Writing Conference: The second decade. *Computers and Composition,* 23(2): 211–27.

Getto, Giuseppe, Cushman, Ellen, & Ghosh, Shreelina. (2011). Community mediation: Writing in communities and enabling connections through new media. *Computers and Composition,* 28(2): 160–74.

González, Jennifer. (2000). The appended subject: Race and identity as digital assemblage. In Beth E. Kolko, Lisa Nakamura, & Gilberg B. Rodman (Eds.), *Race in Cyberspace* (27–50). New York: Routledge.

Gossett, Kathie. (2008). *From manuscript to multimedia: Illuminating memory and re[image]ning composition.* (Doctoral Dissertation). Urbana-Champaign: University of Illinois.

Grasso, Floriana. (2002). Towards computational rhetoric. *Informal Logic: Reasoning and Argumentation in Theory and Practice,* 22(3): http://www.phaenex.uwindsor.ca/ojs/leddy/index.php/informal_logic/article/view/2589.

Gurak, Laura. (1997). *Persuasion and privacy in cyberspace: The online protests over Lotus MarketPlace and the Clipper Chip.* New Haven, CT: Yale University Press.

Gurak, Laura. (2001). *Cyberliteracy: Navigating the Internet with awareness.* New Haven, CT: Yale University Press.

Gurak, Laura, & Lay, Mary (Eds.). (2002). *Research in technical communication.* Westport, CT: Praeger Publishers.

Hajjem, C. et al. (2005). Open access to research increases citation impact. Technical Report, Institut des sciences cognitives, Université du Québec à Montréal.

Hajjem, C., Harnad, S., & Gingras, Y. (2005). Ten-year cross-disciplinary comparison of the growth of open access and how it increases research citation impact. *IEEE Data Engineering Bulletin*, 28(4): 39–47.

Handa, Carolyn (Ed.). (2004). *Visual rhetoric in a digital world: A critical sourcebook*. Boston: Bedford/St. Martin's.

Hart-Davidson, William. (2005). Shaping texts that transform: Toward a rhetoric of objects, relationships, and views. In Carol Lipson & Michael Day (Eds.), *Technical communication and the World Wide Web* (27–42). Mahwah, NJ: Lawrence Erlbaum.

Hart-Davidson, William. (2007). Web 2.0: What technical communicators should know as web users become central producers. *Intercom*, September/October.

Hart-Davidson, William, Carter, Kellie, & Sun, Huatong. (2006). Not merely to do, also to be: Lifestyle interfaces and the expanding scope of usability. Unpublished ms.

Hart-Davidson, William, Zappen, James P., & Halloran, S. Michael. (2005). On the formation of democratic citizens: Rethinking the rhetorical tradition in a digital age. In Richard Graff, Arthur E. Walzer, and Janet M. Atwill (Eds.), *The viability of the rhetorical tradition* (125–40). Albany: State University of New York Press.

Hartson, H. Rex. (1998). Human-computer interaction: Interdisciplinary roots and trends. *Journal of Systems and Software*, 43(2): 103–18.

Haskins, Ekaterina. (2007). Between archive and participation: Public memory in a digital age. *Rhetoric Society Quarterly*, 37: 401–22. doi: 10.1080/ 02773940601086794.

HASTAC Scholars Forum. (2011). Critical code studies. http://hastac.org/forums/ hastac-scholars-discussions/critical-code-studies.

Hauser, Gerard A. (1986). *Introduction to rhetorical theory*. Cambridge, MA: Harper and Row.

Hawisher, Gail E., & LeBlanc, Paul (Eds.). (1992). *Reimagining computers and composition: Teaching and research in a virtual age*. Portsmouth, NH: Boynton/Cook.

Hawisher, Gail E. et al. (1996). *Computers and the teaching of writing in American higher education 1979–1994: A history*. Norwood, NJ: Ablex.

Hawisher, Gail E., & Selfe, Cynthia L. (Eds.). (1991). *Evolving perspectives on computers and composition studies: Questions for the 1990s*. Urbana, IL: NCTE.

Hawk, Byron. (2004). Toward a rhetoric of network (media) culture: Notes on polarities and potentiality. *JAC*, 24(4): 831–50.

Hawk, Byron. (2010). Advanced writing: Digital rhetoric. (Course Syllabus). University of South Carolina. http://cdh.sc.edu/~bhawk/460/index.html.

Heba, Gary. (1997). Hyperrhetoric: Multimedia, literacy, and the future of composition. *Computers and Composition*, 14: 19–44.

Heilker, Paul, & King, Jason. (2010). The rhetorics of online autism advocacy: A case for rhetorical listening. In Stuart Selber (Ed.), *Rhetorics and technologies: New directions in writing and communication* (113–33). Columbia, SC: University of South Carolina Press.

Herring, S. C. et al. (2004). Women and children last: The discursive construction of weblogs. In Laura Gurak et al. (Eds.), *Into the Blogosphere: Rhetoric, Community, and Culture of Weblogs*. Minneapolis: University of Minnesota. http://blog.lib.umn.edu/ blogosphere/women_and_children.html.

Hess, Aaron. (2007). In digital remembrance: Vernacular memory and the rhetorical construction of web memorials. *Media Culture & Society*, 29(5): 812–30. doi: 10.1177/0163443707080539.

Hill, Charles, & Helmers, Marguerite (Eds.). (2004). *Defining visual rhetorics*. Mahwah, NJ: Lawrence Erlbaum.

Hilst, Joshua. (2011). Screen/writing: Time and cinematics in an age of rhetorical memory. (Doctoral Dissertation). Clemson, SC: Clemson University.

Hocks, Mary E. (2003). Understanding visual rhetoric in digital writing environments. *College Composition and Communication, 54*(4): 629–56.

Hodgson, Justin et al. (2011). The importance of undergraduate multimedia: An argument in seven acts. *Kairos: A Journal of Rhetoric, Technology, and Pedagogy,* 16(1): http://kairos.technorhetoric.net/16.1/disputatio/hodgson-et-al/JUMPdisputatio.swf.

Holmevik, Jan Rune, & Haynes, Cynthia. (1999). *MOOniversity: A student's guide to online learning environments.* Boston: Allyn & Bacon.

Holquist, Michael. (1990). *Dialogism: Bakhtin and his world.* New York: Routledge.

Horak, Ray. (2007). *Telecommunications and data communications handbook.* Hoboken, NJ: Wiley & Sons.

Hughes, M. A., & Hayhoe, G. F. (2007). *A research primer for technical communication: Methods, exemplars, and analyses.* New York: Routledge.

Hunt, Kevin. (2003). Establishing a presences on the World Wide Web: A rhetorical approach. *Technical Communication,* 50(4): 519–28.

Hurvitz, Jay. (2006). Spamming me softly with his song. Blog post. http://muse.tau.ac.il/maslool/boidem/boidem117.html.

Huysman, M., & Wulf, V. (2006). IT to support knowledge sharing in communities, towards a social capital analysis. *Journal of Information Technology,* 21(1): 40–51.

Hyland, Ken. (1999). Academic attribution: Citation and the construction of disciplinary knowledge. *Applied Linguistics,* 20(3): 341–67.

Jarratt, Susan. (1991). *Rereading the sophists: Classical rhetoric refigured.* Carbondale: Southern Illinois University Press.

Johnson-Eilola, Johndan. (2008). Communication breakdown: The postmodern space of Google. In Byron Hawk, David M. Rieder, & Ollie Oviedo (Eds.), *Small tech: The culture of digital tools* (110–15). Minneapolis: University of Minnesota Press.

Johnson-Eilola, Johndan. (2010). Among texts. In Stuart Selber (Ed.), *Rhetorics and technologies: New directions in writing and communication* (33–55). Columbia, SC: University of South Carolina Press.

Kalmbach, Jim. (2006). Reading the archives: Ten years of nonlinear (*Kairos*) history. *Kairos: A Journal of Rhetoric, Technology, and Pedagogy,* 11(1): http://kairos.technorhetoric.net/11.1/binder.html?topoi/kalmbach/index.html.

Kaplan, Nancy, & Nelson, Michael. (2000). Determining the publication impact of a digital library. *Journal of the American Society for Information Science,* 51(4): 324–39.

Kichiyoshi, K. et al. (1999). Data visualization for supporting query-based data mining. *Proceedings of the IEEE International Conference on Systems, Man, and Cybernetics,* Volume 5 (888–93). doi: 10.1109/ICSMC.1999.815671.

Kiernan, Michael (Ed.). (2000). *The Oxford Francis Bacon IV: The advancement of learning.* Oxford: Oxford University Press.

Killingsworth, M. Jimmie. (2010). Appeals to the body in eco-rhetoric and techno-rhetoric. In Stuart Selber (Ed.), *Rhetorics and technologies: New directions in writing and communication* (77–93). Columbia, SC: University of South Carolina Press.

Kinney, Thomas J. (2007). *Book of quotations on rhetoric.* Unpublished ms.

Kitalong, Karla et al. (2003). Variations on a theme: The technology autobiography as a versatile writing assignment. In Pamela Takayoshi & Brian Huot (Eds.), *Teaching writing with computers: An introduction* (219–33). Boston: Houghton Mifflin.

Kleinberg, Jon M. (1999). Authoritative sources in a hyperlinked environment. *Journal of the ACM,* 46(5): 604–32.

Kling, George. (2006). The concept of the ecosystem. http://www.globalchange. umich.edu/globalchange1/current/lectures/kling/ecosystem/ecosystem.html.

Krause, Steve. (1996). The immediacy of rhetoric: Definitions, illustrations, and implications. (Doctoral Dissertation). Bowling Green, OH: Bowling Green State University. http://www.emunix.emich.edu/~krause/Diss.

Kreiss, Daniel, Finn, Megan, & Turner, Fred. (2011). The limits of peer production: Some reminders from Max Weber for the network society. *New Media & Society*, 13(2): 243–59.

Kress, Gunther. (2003). *Literacy in the new media age*. London: Routledge.

LaGrandeur, Kevin. (2003). Digital images and classical persuasion. In Mary E. Hocks & Michelle R. Kendrick (Eds.), *Eloquent images: Word and image in the age of new media* (117–36). Cambridge, MA: MIT Press.

Landow, George P. (1991). The rhetoric of hypermedia: Some rules for authors. In Paul Dekmy & George P. Landow (Eds.), *Hypermedia and literary studies*. Cambridge, MA: MIT Press.

Landow, George P. (1992). *Hypertext: The convergence of contemporary critical theory and technology*. Baltimore, MD: Johns Hopkins University Press.

Landow, George P. (Ed.). (1994). *Hyper/Text/Theory*. Baltimore, MD: Johns Hopkins University Press.

Langlois, Ganaele et al. (2009). Networked publics: The double articulation of code and politics on Facebook. *Canadian Journal of Communication*, 34(3): 415–34.

Lanham, Richard. (1992). Digital rhetoric: Theory, practice, and property. In Myron Tuman (Ed.), *Literacy online: The promise (and peril) of reading and writing with computers* (221–43). Pittsburgh, PA: University of Pittsburgh Press.

Lanham, Richard. (1993). *The electronic word: Democracy, technology, and the arts*. Chicago: University of Chicago Press.

Lanham, Richard. (2006). *The economics of attention: Style and substance in the age of information*. Chicago: University of Chicago Press.

Lapadat, Judith C. (2002). Written interaction: A key component in online learning. *Journal of Computer-Mediated Communication*, 7(4): http://jcmc.indiana.edu/vol7/ issue4/lapadat.html.

Larson, Ray. (1996). Bibliometrics of the World Wide Web: An exploratory analysis of the intellectual structure of cyberspace. ASIS 96. http://sherlock.berkeley.edu/ asis96/asis96.html.

Latour, Bruno. (1988). *Science in action: How to follow scientists and engineers through society*. Cambridge, MA: Harvard University Press.

Lauer, Janice M. (2004). *Invention in rhetoric and composition*. West Lafayette, IN: Parlor Press.

Law, John. (1986). The heterogeneity of texts. In Michel Callon, John Law, & Arie Rip (Eds.), *Mapping the Dynamics of Science and Technology* (67–83). London: Macmillan.

Law, John. (1992). Notes on the theory of the actor-network: Ordering, strategy and heterogeneity. *Systems Practice*, 5: 379–93.

Lawrence, Steve, & Giles, C. Lee. (1999). Accessibility of information on the web. *Nature*, 400: 107–109.

Leff, Michael. (1983). The topics of argumentative invention in Latin rhetorical theory from Cicero to Boethius. *Rhetorica*, 1: 23–44.

Lengler, Ralph, & Eppler, Martin. (2007). Towards a periodic table of visualization methods of management. In *2007 Proceedings of the IASTED International Conference on Graphics and Visualization in Engineering* (83–88). Anaheim, CA: Acta Press.

Lessig, Lawrence. (2005). Who is allowed to write? Keynote presentation at the Conference on College Composition and Communication, San Francisco, CA.

Lin, Chanchu. (2007). Organizational website design as a rhetorical situation. *IEEE Transactions on Professional Communication*, 50(1): 35–44.

Lindsay, Stan A. (1998). *Implicit rhetoric: Kenneth Burke's extension of Aristotle's concept of entelechy*. Lanham, MD: University Press of America.

List, Dennis. (2005). *Know your audience: A practical guide to media research*. New Zealand: Original Books. http://www.audiencedialogue.net/kya.html.

Lopes, Fernando, Wooldridge, Michael, & Novais, A. Q. (2008). Negotiation among autonomous computational agents: Principles, analysis and challenges. *Artificial Intelligence Review*, 29: 1–44. doi: 10.1007/s10462–009–9107–8.

Losh, Elizabeth. (2009). *Virtualpolitik: An electronic history of government media-making in a time of war, scandal, disaster, miscommunication, and mistakes*. Cambridge, MA: MIT Press.

Mailloux, Steven. (2002). Re-marking slave bodies: Rhetoric as production and reception. *Philosophy and Rhetoric*, 35(2): 96–119. doi: 10.1353/par.2002.0007.

Manovich, Lev. (2001). *The language of new media*. Cambridge, MA: MIT Press.

Marino, Mark C. (2006). Critical code studies. *Electronic Book Review*. http://www.electronicbookreview.com/thread/electropoetics/codology.

Marino, Mark C. (2010). Critical code studies and the electronic book review: An introduction. *Electronic Book Review*. http://www.electronicbookreview.com/thread/firstperson/ningislanded.

Marx, Karl. (1970). *Introduction: Production, consumption, distribution, exchange (circulation): A contribution to the critique of political economy*. New York: International. http://www.marxists.org/archive/marx/works/1859/critique-pol-economy/appx1.htm.

Marx, Karl. (1977). *Capital: Volume One*. Trans. Ben Fowkes. New York: Vintage Books.

Marx, Karl. (1978). *Capital: Volume Two*. Ed. Friedrich Engels. Trans. David Fernbach. New York: Penguin Books.

McComskey, Bruce. (2002). *Gorgias and the new sophistic rhetoric*. Carbondale: Southern Illinois University Press.

McDaid, John. (1991). Toward an ecology of hypermedia. In Gail Hawisher & Cynthia L. Selfe (Eds.), *Evolving perspectives on computers and composition studies: Questions for the 1990s* (203–23). Urbana, IL: NCTE.

McKee, Heidi, & DeVoss, Dànielle (Eds.). (2007). *Digital writing research*. Cresskill, NJ: Hampton Press.

McKee, Heidi, & Porter, James. (2008). The ethics of digital writing research: A rhetorical approach. *College Composition and Communication*, 59(4): 711–49.

McKiernan, Gerry. (1996). CitedSites(sm): Citation indexing of Web resources. http://www.public.iastate.edu/~CYBERSTACKS/Cited.htm.

McLuhan, Marshall. (1964). *Understanding media: The extensions of man*. New York: McGraw-Hill.

Memmott, Talan. (2000). Toward electracy: A conversation with Gregory Ulmer. *Beehive*, 3(4): http://beehive.temporalimage.com/content_apps34/app_a.html.

Miller, Carolyn R. (1984). Genre as social action. *Quarterly Journal of Speech*, 70: 151–76.

Miller, Mark M., & Riechert, Bonnie P. (1994). Identifying themes via concept mapping: A new method of content analysis. Association for Education in Journalism and Mass Communication Annual Meeting, Atlanta, GA. http://excellent.com.utk.edu/~mmmiller/pestmaps.txt.

Miller, Susan. (1991). *Textual carnivals: The politics of composition.* Carbondale: Southern Illinois University Press.

Moretti, Franco. (2000). Conjectures on world literature. *New Left Review,* 1: 54–68.

Moretti, Franco. (2005). *Graphs, maps, trees: Abstract models for a literary history.* New York: Verso.

Moretti, Franco. (2011). Network theory, plot analysis. *New Left Review,* 68: 80–102.

Moulthrop, Stuart. (1991). Beyond the electronic book: A critique of hypertext rhetoric. Proceedings of the Third ACM Conference on Hypertext, 291–98. doi: 10.1145/122974.123001.

Moulthrop, Stuart. (1994). Shadow of an informand: An experiment in hypertext rhetoric. http://iat.ubalt.edu/moulthrop/hypertexts/hoptext.

Mueller, D. (2009). Clouds, graphs, and maps: Distant reading and disciplinary imagination. (Doctoral Dissertation). Retrieved from ProQuest Dissertations and Theses. (Accession Order No. AAT 3385836).

Murray, Patrick. (1998). Beyond the 'commerce and industry' picture of capital. In Christopher J. Arthur & Geert Reuten (Eds.), *The circulation of capital* (33–66). New York: St. Martin's Press.

Nakamura, Lisa. (2008). *Digitizing race: Visual cultures of the Internet.* Minneapolis: University of Minnesota Press.

Nardi, Bonnie A., & O'Day, Vicki L. (1999). *Information ecologies: Using technology with heart.* Cambridge, MA: MIT Press.

National Council of Teachers of English. (2008). The NCTE definition of 21st century literacies. http://www.ncte.org/positions/statements/21stcentdefinition.

North, Stephen. (1987). *The making of knowledge in composition: Portrait of an emerging field.* Portsmouth, NH: Boynton/Cook.

Ooka, Emi, & Wellman, Barry. (2000). Does social capital pay off more within or between ethnic groups—analyzing job searchers in five Toronto ethnic groups. Research Report to the Toronto Joint Center of Excellence for Research on Immigration and Settlement. http://citeseerx.ist.psu.edu/viewdoc/download?doi=10.1.1.13.2874.

Packer, Randall, & Jordan, Ken. (2001). Overture. In Randall Packer & Ken Jordan (Eds.), *Multimedia: From Wagner to virtual reality* (xv–xxxviii). New York: W. W. Norton.

Park, Han Woo. (2003). Hyperlink network analysis: A new method for the study of social structure on the web. *Connections,* 25(1): 49–61.

Park, Han Woo, & Thelwall, Mike. (2003). Hyperlink analyses of the World Wide Web: A Review. *Journal of Computer-Mediated Communication,* 8(4): http://jcmc.indiana.edu/vol8/issue4/park.html.

Pashaei, Fatima H. (2010). Unstable situations: A rhetorical approach to studying blogs about Muslims. (Master's Thesis). Fairfax, VA: George Mason University.

Pawlett, William. (2007). *Jean Baudrillard: Against banality.* New York: Routledge.

Pentzold, Christian. (2010). Imagining the Wikipedia community: What do Wikipedia authors mean when they write about their 'community'? *New Media & Society,* 13(5): 704–21.

Perelman, Chaim. (1982). *The realm of rhetoric.* Notre Dame, IN: University of Notre Dame Press.

Perelman, Chaim, & Olbrechts-Tyteca, Lucie. (1969). *The new rhetoric: A treatise on argumentation.* Trans. John Wilkinson & Purcell Weaver. Notre Dame, IN: University of Notre Dame Press.

Pfister, Damien. (2011). The Logos of the blogosphere: Flooding the zone, invention, and attention in the Lott imbroglio. *Argument and Advocacy*, 47: 141–62.

Pickett, S. T. A., & Cadenasso, M. L. (2002). The ecosystem as a multidimensional concept: Meaning, model, and metaphor. *Ecosystems*, 5: 1–10.

Porter, James E. (2002). Why technology matters to writing: A cyberwriter's tale. *Computers and Composition*, 20(3): 375–94.

Porter, James E. (2005). The rhetoric of digital delivery: Access, interaction, economics. Conference on College Composition and Communication, San Francisco, CA.

Porter, James E. (2007). Foreword. In Heidi McKee and Dànielle DeVoss (Eds.), *Digital writing research* (ix-xix). New York: Hampton Press.

Porter, James E. (2009). Recovering delivery for digital rhetoric. *Computers and Composition*, 26(4): 207–24. doi: 10.1016/j.compcom.2009.09.004.

Porter, James E. (2010). Rhetoric in (as) a digital economy. In Stuart Selber (Ed.), *Rhetorics and technologies: New directions in writing and communication* (173—97). Columbia, SC: University of South Carolina Press.

Porter, James E., & Sullivan, Patricia. (1994). Repetition and the rhetoric of visual design. In Barbara Johnstone (Ed.), *Repetition in discourse: Interdisciplinary perspectives* (114–29). Vol. 2. Norwood, NJ: Ablex.

Potts, Liza. (2009). Using Actor Network Theory to trace and improve multimodal communication design. *Technical Communication Quarterly*, 18(3): 281–301.

Prior, Paul et al. (2007). Re-situating and re-mediating the canons: A Cultural-historical remapping of rhetorical activity. *Kairos: A Journal of Rhetoric, Technology, and Pedagogy* 11(3): http://kairos.technorhetoric.net/11.3/binder.html?topoi/prior-et-al/index.html.

Recknagel, Friedrich. (1989). *Applied systems ecology: Approach and case studies in aquatic ecology.* Berlin: Akademie-Verlag.

Reed, Chris, & Norman, Timothy (Eds.). (2004). *Argumentation machines: New frontiers in argumentation and computation.* Dordrecht, The Netherlands: Kluwer Academic Publishers.

Reed, Scott. (2009). Extra lives, extra limbs: Videogaming, cybernetics, and rhetoric after "literacy." (Doctorial Dissertation). Athens: University of Georgia.

Reilly, Colleen, & Eyman, Douglas. (2007). Multifaceted methods for multi-modal texts: Alternate approaches to citation analysis for electronic sources. In Heidi McKee and Dànielle DeVoss (Eds.), *Digital writing research* (353–76). New York: Hampton Press.

Reputation.com. (2011). http://www.reputation.com.

Rheingold, Howard. (1993). *The virtual community: Homesteading on the electronic frontier.* New York: Addison Wesley.

Rheingold, Howard. (2002). *Smart mobs: The next social revolution.* Cambridge, MA: Basic Books.

Rice, Jeff. (2006). Networks and new media. *College English*, 69(2): 127–33.

Rice, Jeff. (2010). English <A>. In Bradley Dilger and Jeff Rice (Eds.), *From A to <A>: Kewords in markup* (49–66). Minneapolis: University of Minnesota Press.

Richards, I. A. (1930). *Practical criticism: A study of literary judgment.* London: Kegan Paul, Trench, Tubner & Co.

Ridolfo, James. (2005). Rhetoric, economy and the technology of actvist delivery. (Masters Thesis). East Lansing: Michigan State University.

Ridolfo, James. (2006). (C).omprehensive (O).nline (D).ocument (E).valuation. *Kairos:*

A Journal of Rhetoric, Technology, and Pedagogy, 10(2): http://kairos.technorhetoric. net/10.2/binder.html?praxis/ridolfo/index.html.

Ridolfo, James, & DeVoss, Dànielle Nicole. (2009). Composing for recomposition: Rhetorical velocity and delivery. *Kairos: A Journal of Rhetoric, Technology, and Pedagogy*, 13(2): http://kairos.technorhetoric.net/13.2/topoi/ridolfo_devoss/velocity.html.

Riley, Brendan. (2010). A style guide to the secrets of <style>. In Bradley Dilger and Jeff Rice (Eds.), *From A to <A>: Kewords in markup* (67–80). Minneapolis: University of Minnesota Press.

Roberts, C. W. (2001). Content analysis. In N. J. Smelser & P. B. Baltes (Eds.), *International encyclopedia of the social and behavioral sciences*. Vol. 4 (2697–2702). London: Pergamon Press.

Robillard, Amy E. (2006). Young scholars affecting composition: A challenge to disciplinary citation practices. *College English*, 68(3): 253–70.

Rogers, E. M. (1987). Progress, problems and prospects for network research: Investigating relationships in the age of electronic communication technologies. *Social Networks*, 9: 285–310.

Romberger, Julia. (2007). An ecofeminist methodology: Studying the ecological dimensions of the digital environment. In Heidi McKee & Dànielle DeVoss (Eds.), *Digital writing research* (248–68). New York: Hampton Press.

Rousseau, Ronald. (1997). Sitations: An exploratory study. *Cybermetrics*, 1(1): http://www.cindoc.csic.es/cybermetrics/articles/v1i1p1.html.

Salvo, Michael J., & Doherty, Mick. (2002). Kairos: past, present and future(s). *Kairos: A Journal of Rhetoric, Technology, and Pedagogy*, 7(x): http://kairos.technorhetoric. net/7.x/binder.html?kairos/title.htm.

Sauer, Beverly. (2003). *The rhetoric of risk: Technical documentation in hazardous environments*. Mahwah, NJ: Lawrence Erlbaum.

Scott, John. (1991). *Social network analysis: A handbook*. London: Sage.

Scott, Linda. (1994). Images in advertising: The need for a theory of visual rhetoric. *Journal of Consumer Research*, 21(2): 252–73.

Selber, Stuart. (2004). *Multiliteracies for a digital age*. Carbondale: Southern Illinois University Press.

Selfe, Cynthia. (2004). Students who teach us: A case study of a new media text designer. In Anne Wysocki et al., *Writing new media: Theory and applications for expanding the teaching of composition* (43–66). Logan: Utah State University Press.

Selfe, Cynthia, & Hawisher, Gail (Eds.). (2004). *Literate lives in the information age: Narratives of literacy from the United States*. Mahwah, NJ: Lawrence Erlbaum.

Shannon, Claude. (1948). A mathematical theory of communication. *Bell Systems Technical Journal*, 27: 379–423, 623–56.

Shannon, Claude, & Weaver, Warren. (1949). *The mathematical theory of communication*. Urbana-Champaign: University of Illinois Press.

Simondon, Gilbert. (1989). *L'individuation psychique et collective: À la lumiére des notions de forme, information, potentiel et métastabilité*. Paris: Aubier.

Skeen, Thomas. (2009). The rhetoric of human-computer interaction. In Susan Miller-Cochran & Rochelle Rodgrio (Eds.), *Rhetorically rethinking usability: Theories, practices, and methodologies* (91–104). Cresskill, NJ: Hampton Press.

Skinnell, Ryan. (2010). Circuitry in motion: Rhetoric(al) moves in YouTube's archive. *Enculturation*, 8: http://enculturation.gmu.edu/circuitry-in-motion.

Slack, Jennifer, Miller, David, & Doak, Jeffrey. (1993). The technical communicator as author: Meaning, power, authority. *Journal of Business and Technical Communication*, 7: 12–36.

Small, Henry. (1999). A passage through science: Crossing disciplinary boundaries. *Library Trends*, 48(1): 72–108.

Software Studies Initiative. (2007). Software studies. http://lab.softwarestudies. com/2007/05/about-software-studies-ucsd.html.

Spinuzzi, Clay. (2003). *Tracing genres through organizations: A sociocultural approach to information design*. Cambridge, MA: MIT Press.

Spinuzzi, Clay, & Zachary, Mark. (2000). Genre ecologies: An open system approach to understanding and constructing documentation. *Journal of Computer Documentation*, 24(3): 169–81.

Sterling, Bruce. (2005). *Shaping things*. Cambridge, MA: MIT Press.

Sullivan, Patricia, & Porter, James E. (1993). Remapping curricular geography: Professional Writing in/and English. *Journal of Business and Technical Communication*, 7(4): 389–422.

Sullivan, Patricia, & Porter, James E. (1997). *Opening spaces: Writing technologies and critical research practices*. Greenwich, CT: Ablex.

Swarts, J. (2008). Information technologies as discursive agents: Methodological implications for the empirical study of knowledge work. *Journal of Technical Writing and Communication*, 38(4): 301–29.

Syverson, Margaret. (1999). *The wealth of reality: An ecology of composition*. Carbondale: Southern Illinois University Press.

Taylor, Mark C. (2003). *The moment of complexity: Emerging network culture*. Chicago: University of Chicago Press.

Taylor, Paul. (1992). Social epistemic rhetoric and chaotic discourse. In Gail Hawisher & Paul LeBlanc (Eds.), *Reimagining computers and composition: Teaching and research in a virtual age* (131–48). Portsmouth, NH: Boynton/Cook.

Taylor, Todd, & Ward, Irene (Eds.). (1998). *Literacy theory in the age of the Internet*. New York: Columbia University Press.

Terranova, Tiziana. (2004). *Network culture: Politics for the information age*. London: Pluto Press.

Titscher, Stefan et al. (2000). *Methods of text and discourse analysis*. London: Sage.

Tomlinson, Elizabeth. (2011). Conceptualizing audience in digital invention. (Doctorial Dissertation). Kent, OH: Kent State University.

Toulmin, Stephen. (1969). *The Uses of Argument*. Cambridge: Cambridge University Press.

Trimbur, John. (2000). Composition and the circulation of writing. *College Composition and Composition*, 52: 188–219.

Tuman, Myron (Ed.). (1992). *Literacy online: The promise (and peril) of reading and writing with computers*. Pittsburgh, PA: University of Pittsburgh Press.

Turkle, Sherry. (1995). *Life on the screen: Identity in the age of the Internet*. New York: Simon & Schuster.

Turnley, Melinda. (2011). Towards a mediological method: A framework for critically engaging dimensions of a medium. *Computers and Composition*, 28(2): 126–44.

Ulmer, Gregory. (1989). *Teletheory: Grammatology in the age of video*. New York: Routledge.

Ulmer, Gregory. (2003). *Internet invention: From literacy to electracy*. New York: Longman.

van Dijk, J. (2009). Users like you? Theorizing agency in user-generated content. *Media, Culture, & Society*, 31(1): 41–58.

Van House, Nancy. (2001). Actor-network theory, knowledge work, and digital libraries. http://www.sims.berkeley.edu/~vanhouse/bridge.html.

Vatz, Richard E. (1973). The myth of the rhetorical situation. *Philosophy and Rhetoric*, 6(3): 154–61.

Walker, Joyce. (2002). Textural textuality: A personal exploration of critical race theory. *Kairos: A Journal of Rhetoric, Technology, and Pedagogy*, 7(1): http://kairos.technorheto ric.net/7.1/binder.html?features/walker/text/index.html.

Walker, Joyce. (2006). Hyper.activity. *Kairos: A Journal of Rhetoric, Technology, and Pedagogy*, 10(2): http://kairos.technorhetoric.net/10.2/binder2.html?coverweb/walker/index.html.

Walpole, Jane R. (1981). Ramus revisited: The uses and limits of classical rhetoric. JAC, 2(1–2): http://jac.gsu.edu/jac/2/Articles/7.htm.

Walter, John. (2005). Notes from the Walter J. Ong archives. Wednesday, May 04, 2005. http://johnwalter.blogspot.com/2005/05/ive-mentioned-fact-that-our-plan-is-to.html.

Warnick, Barbara. (2007). *Rhetoric online: Persuasion and politics on the World Wide Web.* New York: Peter Lang.

Wasserman, S., & Faust, K. (1994). *Social network analysis: Methods and applications.* Cambridge, UK: Cambridge University Press.

Welch, Kathleen E. (1999). *Electric rhetoric: Classical rhetoric, oralism, and a new literacy.* Cambridge, MA: MIT Press.

Wellman, Barry. (1997). An electronic group is virtually a social network. In S. Kiesler (Ed.), *The culture of the Internet* (179–208). Mahwah, NJ: Lawrence Erlbaum.

Wellman, Barry. (2003). A non-technical introduction to social network analysis. Sunbelt Social Network Conference, February 2003. http://www.chass.utoronto.ca/~wellman/publications/networksfornewbies/networks4newbies.ppt.

Wellman, Barry. (2004). The three ages of Internet Studies: Ten, five and zero years ago. *New Media & Society*, 6(1): 123–29.

Wellman, Barry, & Berkowitz, S. D. (Eds.). (1988). *Social structure: A network approach.* Cambridge, UK: Cambridge University Press.

White, Howard D., & McCain, Katherine W. (1998). Visualizing a discipline: An author co-citation analysis of information science, 1972–1995. *Journal of the American Society for Information Science*, 49(4): 327–55.

Whittemore, Stewart. (2008). Metadata and memory: Lessons from the canon of memoria for the design of content management systems. *Technical Communication Quarterly*, 17(1): 88–109.

WIDE Research Center Collective. (2005). Why teach digital writing? *Kairos: A Journal of Rhetoric, Technology, and Pedagogy*, 10(1): http://kairos.technorhetoric.net/10.1/binder2.html?coverweb/wide/index.html.

Williams, Sean. (2008). Dreamweaver and the procession of simulations: What you see is not why you get what you get. In Byron Hawk, David M. Rieder, & Ollie Oviedo (Eds.), *Small tech: The culture of digital tools* (57–68). Minneapolis: University of Minnesota Press.

Wojcik, Michael. (2011). Estimating sentiment in ELI: Computational analysis of tone in student responses to student writing. http://ideoplast.org/al841/eli-sentiment.pdf.

Wysocki, Anne Frances. (2002). A bookling monument. *Kairos: A Journal of Rhetoric, Technology, and Pedagogy*, 7(3): http://kairos.technorhetoric.net/7.3/binder2.html?coverweb/wysocki/index.htm.

Wysocki, Anne Frances. (2004). Opening new media to writing: Openings and justifications. In Anne Wysocki et al., *Writing new media: Theory and applications for expanding the teaching of composition* (1–42). Logan: Utah State University Press.

Yancey, Kathleen Blake (Ed.). (2006). *Delivering college composition: The fifth canon.* Portsmouth, NH: Boynton/Cook.

Young, Richard, Becker, Alton, & Pike, Kenneth. (1970). *Rhetoric: Discovery and change.* New York: Harcourt, Brace, & World.

Zan, Luca, Zambon, Stefano, & Pettigrew, Andrew. (1993). *Perspectives on strategic change.* New York: Springer.

Zappen, James P. (2005). Digital rhetoric: Toward an integrated theory. *Technical Communication Quarterly*, 14(3): 319–25.

Zappen, James, Gurak, Laura, & Doheny-Farina, Stephen. (1997). Rhetoric, community, and cyberspace. *Rhetoric Review*, 15(2): 400–19. doi: 10.1080/07350199709359226.

Zoetewey, Meredith. (2010). A rhetoric of ornament: Decorating mobile devices in the aesthetic economy. *Computers and Composition*, 27(2): 138–57.

Index